Based Deleuze

Based Deleuze

The Reactionary Leftism of
Gilles Deleuze

Justin Murphy, Ph.D.

Table of Contents

Preface

I have tried to write a short and accessible book about the French philosopher Gilles Deleuze (1925-1995). This book was conceived and written in one immanent movement, from July 20th to August 20th, 2019.

An unexpected benefit of publishing at the speed of cyberspace is that many of my most scathing critics wrote public reviews before I even started writing. Where they obtained the predictive power to comment on a book not yet written, I do not know. But thanks to their generous public sharing, I had the opportunity to systematically pre-empt and hopefully resolve all of the major critiques and objections that this book would otherwise tend to elicit.

This book does not intend to provide a comprehensive and balanced portrait of Deleuze's thought. Critics will accuse me of cherry-picking quotes, running roughshod over crucial contextual factors, and ignoring much of the scholarly literature, to produce an absurd and politically motivated image of Deleuze. They will not be entirely wrong! This book is just one portrait, from one angle, of a rich and complex body of work. Of course, it is motivated by my own interests and desires. Of course, it only exposes one slice of its object — this is probably the only worthwhile way to write about another thinker. And it is certainly the only kind of "secondary literature" (writing about someone else's writing), that anyone would ever choose to read for stimulation and edification. For most of modern intellectual history, this was typically *expected* of any commentary worth its salt. Only today does there exist a peanut gallery capable of objecting to such an approach, a consequence of the massification of higher education.

Scholarly norms in the humanities today are morbid to the extreme, as their evolution in the past few decades has been driven primarily by the need to filter out increasing applicants. This pressure has laced them with more and more resentment. Any piece of academic commentary must first cite at least a few dozen pieces of recent scholarly integration is just too great to bear, it seems. Resentful at the years they wasted paying dues, now they feel nothing but revulsion at the sight of intellectual life that has ceased to pay its dues. They cling to the most dejected and disingenuous peripheries of an Academy that has not only mercilessly stultified them but no longer even pretends to offer them anything now or in the future. Rather than realize this, update their model of the world, defect from a rotten game, and get to work both enjoying and producing the bizarre fruits of the Outside, they specialize in *objecting*.

Critique is well and good, but when people *object* to the existence of a book, whether that objection is one of "cherry-picking" or being "pseudo-intellectual" or whatever — they only announce themselves members of this morbid para-academic peanut gallery, this informal labor union of resentful retards rearranging deck chairs on the Titanic. Now that this peanut gallery has been explained, they can be safely ignored.

Perhaps the most reasonable critique of my portrait of Deleuze is what scientists call *face invalidity*. That's a fancy way of saying it just sounds wrong, or fails the "sniff test;" it's too incongruous with too many obvious facts, that it's implausible just on the face of it. As I discuss in the chapter *On Troubled Land,* I initially rejected Nick Land's pro-capitalist portrait of Deleuze on grounds of face invalidity. Deleuze had explicitly endorsed too many notions, principles, and causes of left-wing anti-capitalism for Land's Deleuze to be plausible. In that chapter, I explain how and why my rejection gave way to a certain recalibration of my beliefs, so I won't rehearse that story here. Suffice it to say that I respect why many readers will be similarly skeptical of the Deleuze they meet in the following pages.

If my portrait of Deleuze seems impossible on the face of it, then perhaps we should inquire into who or what has generated the face of Deleuze we currently take for granted. Even the quickest look at the academic consensus on Deleuze will make any reader far less confident in whatever they've already heard about Deleuze. Consider the following masterpieces of scholarship one might find conducting research on Deleuze:

- *Un-Glunking Geography: Spatial Science After Dr. Seuss and Gilles Deleuze* (Doel 2002)

- *Deleuze and Guattari in the Nursery: Towards an Ethnographic, Multi-Sensory Mapping of Gendered Bodies and Becomings* (Emma and Mellor 2013)

- *Becoming Rhizomatic Parents: Deleuze, Guattari and Disabled Babies* (Goodley 2007)

- *'Ecosystem Service Commodities' - a New Imperial Ecology? Implications for Animist Immanent Ecologies, With Deleuze and Guattari* (Sullivan 2010)

- *Immaculate Defecation: Gilles Deleuze and Félix Guattari in Organization Theory* (Sørensen 2005)

- *Virtually Sustainable: Deleuze and Desiring Differenciation in Second Life* (Hickey-Moody and Wood 2008)

- *Transgender Without Organs? Mobilizing a Geo-Affective Theory of Gender Modification* (Crawford 2008)

- *Deleuze on Viagra (Or, What Can a 'Viagra-Body' Do?)* (Potts 2004)

Do these titles inspire confidence? Do you believe the institutionalized culture generating these titles would likely impart to the public an accurate and useful image of a complicated French

7

philosopher? And yet... Most of what you think you know about Deleuze has come to you, through osmosis, from the same kind of geniuses who crafted these titles.

Deleuze was ensconced in a left-wing milieu but, like many great philosophers, he regularly transgressed the boundaries of his putative ideological identity. He frequently promoted vitalism, despite its fascist connotations. With Friedrich Nietzsche he rejects the "Blank Slate" theory — now effectively mandatory in the academic humanities — that all psychological and behavioral differences across humans are due only to different environmental conditions; he seems to affirm the role played by heritable genetic endowments in the emergence of objective and legitimate social hierarchies. There is some indication he believes in "race realism," as he stresses the significance of racial delirium in schizophrenia and even calls on his readers to *purify their race.* Guattari was frequently conducting psychotherapeutic experiments with the mentally ill but, in the words of Eugene Wolters, Deleuze "hated crazy people" (2013). In contrast to the relativism that dominates contemporary philosophy, Deleuze followed the 13th-century Catholic priest Duns Scotus in affirming the univocity of being. For Deleuze, everything is composed of one divine substance. Finally, collective liberation is a real prospect for Deleuze but, contrary to the secular-atheist drift of twentieth-century radical leftism, his ultimate vision for social revolution points "out of this world" (Hallward 2006).

Whenever I tell people that Deleuze was curiously reactionary for a radical-left philosopher, nobody seems to have any idea what I'm talking about. Now there is at least one book I can give them.[1]

---

[1] For other books, podcasts, and videos, see my curated list of resources at theotherlifenow.com/deleuze-resources.

Chapter One

Some Terminology

Deleuze was a *post-structuralist* but he was not, as many presume, a *postmodernist.* "Postmodernism" is typically used as a catch-all pejorative to name the generalized rootlessness, fragmentation, and incoherence characteristic of Western culture today. Post-structuralism is often associated with postmodernism because they sound similar, their most famous representatives are French, and they seem to have both kicked into high gear sometime from about the 1970s. As a result, most people who hear of post-structuralism assume it's a bunch of highfalutin French charlatans peddling absurd concepts. Names likely to be mentioned as exemplars include Michel Foucault, Jacques Derrida, and... Gilles Deleuze. Thus, to the degree

Deleuze rings a bell to normal people, it is a bell that sounds like postmodernism: rootlessness, fragmentation, and incoherence.

It's a particularly unfortunate mistake, however, because Deleuze provides more possible exits from the postmodern impasse than any other philosopher since World War II.

Post-structuralism refers to a cluster of quite diverse intellectual projects. All they had in common was a general drift away from the dominant style of the preceding period — structuralism — as exemplified by Claude Lévi-Strauss in anthropology, Ferdinand de Saussure in linguistics, and Louis Althusser in philosophy. We don't need a long detour into structuralism; suffice it to say that the spirit of structuralism was proud, stodgy, and overly pleased with its own rigor — or rather its *aesthetics* of rigor. Althusser, for instance, genuinely believed that Karl Marx discovered *the* science of history, on par with the discoveries of Galileo (1990). The only way to avoid the traps of bourgeois ideology, according to Althusser, is to follow Althusser's voluminous, scientistic interpretive dictates.[2] It was inevitable that some cheeky upstarts with poetic flare would eventually launch their own careers by deflating these stuffy windbags (did I mention that Althusser murdered his wife?). To be honest, none of this really matters, which *is* what matters: the label "post-structuralist" tells you close to nothing about what someone thinks. It might sound like postmodernism, but it's really just a vague stylistic tendency in France in the last third of the twentieth century.

Post-structuralists such as Foucault and Deleuze are now widely seen as "cultural Marxists" — thanks to a popular talking point of the Canadian psychologist Jordan Peterson — implying that their philosophies are merely vehicles for class war. Yet during the heydays of post-structuralism, figures such as Foucault and Deleuze were more likely to be seen as traitors to Marxism. Recall that it was not until 1956 that Jean-Paul Sartre — the most towering intellectual figure of twentieth-century France — finally disavowed the Soviet Union.

---

[2] *Reading Marx* (Althusser and Balibar 2009) is at once more esoteric and more triumphalist than Marx's own writings.

Deleuze wrote his first book (on David Hume) in 1953. Post-structuralism was not an adaptive mutation of economic Marxism onto the cultural plane so much as a defiant assertion of autonomy and creativity *away from Marxism*.

To propose an examination of "reactionary" components within the work of a "left-wing post-structuralist" is — when seen in this light — not as scandalous as my critics suggest.

As I will try to show, the work of Gilles Deleuze furnishes a number of antidotes to the chaotic evils of postmodernism. There remains a widespread impression that Deleuze was a chaotic thinker, promoting absurd and ridiculous concepts to smash rigid and traditional norms. In fact, I believe Deleuze wanted to subvert precisely postmodern tendencies, for instance, the tendency to be distracted by arbitrary and fleeting fashions, or to be captured by marketers and algorithms. He wanted to cut through what he called all of our "false problems," to show that in every passing moment there is only one, pure, uninterrupted past, working through us.

The Two Meanings of "Reaction"

Discussing the ideological valence of great thinkers is difficult because they have little use for the crutches of ideology. The difficulty is particularly acute today, when ideological labels are used so loosely, and often with ulterior motives. I should therefore clarify, at the outset, what I mean by "reactionary" in the subtitle of this book.

In some sense, Deleuze was explicitly anti-reactionary. He was anti-reactionary in the sense that he was *anti-reactive,* in the spirit of Baruch Spinoza and Nietzsche. To be a reactionary, in this pejorative sense, means to be always responding to active, superior forces, instead of becoming an active force; to be captured by sad affects, to be resentful, and to think and act with these as one's motive forces. This common sense understanding of reactionism partially maps onto the modern political-ideological sense of the word. The data show that conservatives are more reactive to disgusting stimuli, for instance (Inbar, Pizarro, and Bloom 2009). Experiments have shown that even just the presence of foul odors can make people

14

slightly, but measurably, more conservative (Schnall et al. 2008). Conservatives are more likely to see threats and reactively demand "law and order." Edmund Burke watched the French Revolution with horror, and famously wrote about his reactions. Henceforth, we'll refer to this aspect of reactionary or conservative politics as *reactivism.* I prefer *reactivism* to *reactionism* because it will remind us that left-wing progressive *activism* is much closer to this sense of "reactionary" than we are accustomed to thinking. Reactionary politics in this sense, *reactivism*, can be a failure mode of left-wing politics no less than right-wing politics.

Things get confusing because modern society also calls reactionary *whatever transgresses left-wing or progressive norms.* Nietzsche, for instance, is seen by many as a reactionary, even though one pillar of his whole life's philosophy is a contempt for reactive tendencies. From the twentieth century, and especially after World War II, any sufficiently disagreeable and strong-willed individual eager to avoid reactivism — who wishes to constitute an authentic, healthy, and autonomous existence — will eventually be coded as reactionary. Even if their political beliefs are ideologically ambiguous or ambivalent. Thus, individual intellectuals as diverse as Ernst Jünger, the Italian Futurists, Martin Heidegger, Salvador Dalí, Jack Kerouac, and even Hunter S. Thompson would all earn the distinction (to varying degrees).[3] Strong and uncompromisingly *active* drives get coded as "reactionary" if the individual is not plausibly linked to the larger collective liberation struggle of some officially marginalized group. It is only in this sense of the term that we will find a "reactionary" component in the philosophy of Deleuze.

This latter sense of "reaction" is a recurring, subterranean tendency that can arise from the Left as well as the Right. It is most likely to emerge from the Right, but in periods when "the Left" becomes especially decadent, the responsibility to transgress "the Left" will occasionally fall to an otherwise proper leftist. There is evidence that Deleuze was writing in such a context. Deleuze's first explicitly political book with Félix Guattari

---

[3] On Hunter S. Thompson, who was explicitly and actively aligned with the Left throughout his life, see Poulous (2005).

16

was published in 1972. Only two years later, under a well-documented Deleuzo-Guattarian influence, Jean-François Lyotard published what he would later call his "evil book" (1990). *Libidinal Economy* is arguably more favorable to capitalism than Deleuzo-Guattarian accelerationism. Adding insult to injury, Lyotard seems to blame the workers for their own oppression. One would need a whole book to fully explore all of the subtle currents of reactionary leftism in postwar European philosophy. Suffice it to say that Deleuze's reactionary leftism was not a random or isolated fluke, but rather comprehensible in its context — and even repeated, to some degree, by Lyotard.

17

Chapter Two

On Troubled Land

When I first heard about Nick Land's commercialist reading of Deleuze, I thought he was joking. According to Land, the enigmatic Deleuzian concept of "deterritorialization" — a popular *cri de cœur* among angsty collegiate poet-revolutionaries — is essentially reducible to *entrepreneurship* (Land 2013; Murphy 2017a). According to Land, Deleuze believes the market is the engine of what leftists would call emancipation or liberation (to whatever degree there is emancipation and liberation on the horizon for Deleuze, a question to which we will return in the final chapter). As we will see, I still believe it's implausible to understand Deleuze as a straightforward lover of capitalism. Deleuze has made far too many remarks to the

Deleuze was a leftist insofar as he wanted to see power over property and contracts more equally distributed and decentralized. But this is a widespread preference, so it's not very interesting. More interesting is how little this revolutionary philosopher espoused the antinomian politics fashionable at the time: from militant protest, to overthrowing traditional family structures, to the anti-capitalist and anti-imperialist kidnappings and bombings and airplane highjackings common in the 1970s, etc. He is known to have signed a few petitions, but in such a radical and mobilized milieu as his, signing a few petitions indicates a curious detachment. In my view, Deleuze's political behavior looks like an overwhelmingly disinterested person doing the bare minimum to not flagrantly insult his punch-drunk peer group. Not to mention that petitions are a rather pronomian political behavior — seeking a change to the nomos, but by respecting the protocols of the nomos.

Although Deleuze wanted to see power equally distributed, the shockingly under-recognized fact is that Deleuze was a radical *pronomian.* He was obsessed with the social technology of *contracts,* and especially their creative and liberatory potential. Consider the following from his interview with the much more antinomian theorist and militant Antonio Negri:

> *I was initially more interested in law than politics. Even with Masoch and Sade what I liked was the thoroughly twisted conception of contracts in Masoch, and of institutions in Sade, as these come out in relation to sexuality. And in the present day, I see Francois Ewald's work to reestablish a philosophy of law as quite fundamental. What interests me isn't the law or laws (the former being an empty notion, the latter uncritical notions), nor even law or rights, but jurisprudence. It's jurisprudence, ultimately, that creates law, and we mustn't go on leaving this to judges. Writers ought to read law reports rather than the Civil Code. People are already thinking about establishing a system of law for modern biology; but everything in modern biology and the new situations it creates, the new courses of events it makes possible, is a matter for jurisprudence. We don't need an ethical committee of supposedly well-qualified wise men, but user-groups. This is where we move from law into politics (Negri and Deleuze 1990).*

As Moldbug notes, antinomianism supplies a crucial *adaptive morbidity* to the contagious and highly successful memeplex of secular progressivism (technically the most recent atheist mutation of Protestantism, exemplified by Richard Dawkins' replacement of *The God Delusion* with a mystical zeitgeist of liberal progress). A majority will find it highly attractive to remove all hard constraints on resource transfers, though such a non-principle is also doomed to destroy any system. If law is not sacred, resources can be transferred from anyone to anyone else, at any time, according to any principle that is fashionable or favored by those with power.

It turns out, therefore, no intelligent and honest leftist can consciously endorse pure antinomianism, for antinomianism will ultimately reflect the Thrasymachian position that "might equals right." Instead, modern leftists since Marx somewhat consciously opt for an instrumentally justified dishonesty: publicly moralize about the evils of unbridled domination, tell everyone that "might does not equal right," but organize the masses precisely on the claim that *their* might will make right. This also explains why most Marxist revolutions become fascist in the end, for their practical logic is based on a contradictory, mobilizing shell game. Antinomian before taking power, pronomian after taking power. In the end, one realizes that the most perfect antinomianism is *capitalism.* The meaning of any word whatsoever can be changed overnight, with enough entrepreneurial creativity. All that is solid melts into air, as Marx put it.

It would seem to follow that a consistent and honest leftism requires at least some component of reactionary pronomianism, but before "the revolution." This is how we will understand Deleuze's seemingly strange interest in law and contracts. To explain what I mean, we must first take a detour down the road of sexual pathology. For it is on questions of sexual pathology that Deleuze first cuts his teeth on the question of jurisprudence.

In *Coldness and Cruelty* (1989), a book about the concept of "sado-masochism," Deleuze ultimately rejects the idea that sadism and masochism are two poles of one dimension.

26

Through philosophical readings of Marquis de Sade and Leopold Von Sacher-Masoch, Deleuze argues that a masochist will never be fully satisfied with a sadist as his torturer, and a sadist cannot maximize his pleasure on a willing masochist. Whereas masochism is all about Law and contracts, the sadist hates contracts (pp. 76).

In short, sadism is *antinomian* and masochism is *pronomian*. The preferred political vehicle for the antinomian progressive is the norm or *institution,* whereas the preferred political vehicle for the pronomian is the *contract.* Following the French revolutionary Saint-Just, the Marquis de Sade explicitly favored a radical institutionalism that would have done with all laws. Deleuze explicates the political coordinates of institutions versus contracts perfectly in the following passage, which deserves to be quoted at length.

> *The juridical distinction between contract and institution is well known: the contract presupposes in principle the free consent of the contracting parties and determines between them a system of reciprocal rights and duties; it cannot affect a third party and is valid for a limited period. Institutions, by*

contrast, determine a long-term state of affairs which is both involuntary and inalienable; it establishes a power or an authority which takes effect against a third party. But even more significant is the difference between the contract and the institution with respect to what is known as a law: the contract actually generates a law, even if this law oversteps and contravenes the conditions which made it possible; the institution is of a very different order in that it tends to render laws unnecessary, to replace the system of rights and duties by a dynamic model of action, authority and power. Saint-Just accordingly demanded that there should be many institutions and few laws, and proclaimed that the Republic could not be a republic so long as laws had the supremacy over institutions... In short, the specific impulse underlying the contract is toward the creation of a law, even if in the end the law should take over and impose its authority upon the contract itself; whereas the corresponding impulse at work in the case of the institution is toward the degradation of all laws and the establishment of a superior power that sets itself above them (pp. 77).

Though *Coldness and Cruelty* maintains a neutral analytical tone befitting a professional philosopher, it is easy to see that masochism is more neatly aligned with Deleuze's own worldview and character. Sadism points "upward" toward a "transcendent higher principle (pp. 88)," ironically demonstrating the cruelty inherent in enlightenment rationality. Masochism instead points "downward" toward an immanent diversion of rationality's cruelty, which humorously converts its oppression into pleasure by applying it to oneself with an "excess of zeal" (pp. 88). Sadism is more compressed and hurried, whereas masochism is drawn out and relies on waiting (Reynolds 2006, 97–98). Remember that slowness is privileged in Deleuze's works with Guattari, as a way of going fast (1987, 499). And as Reynolds points out, Deleuze especially admired writers such as Beckett and Proust, both of whom are known for a "masochistic" sense of time. Reynolds even argues that, broadly speaking, analytic philosophy tends toward sadism and continental philosophy tends toward masochism. In short, everything suggests that, if we wish to draw out a Deleuzian politics of Law, we should look to Masoch *contra* Sade.

When Deleuze tells Negri he is interested in "user-groups" generating their own jurisprudence, he is clearly signaling his affinity with Masoch rather than Sade. He is not asking that we let loose unconstrained authority and power via informal institutions: "We don't need an ethical committee of supposedly well-qualified wise men." Rather he is suggesting that autonomous groups should begin to generate their own Law, with defined parameters, "free consent," no imposition on third parties, etc.

And what we find in masochism is that individuals and small groups can adopt seemingly reactionary and oppressive technologies — Law, contracts, punishments, etc. — as a pathway to liberating revolutionary potential. The masochist seeks to create a novel, sustainable, and collectively empowering combination of cold masculine rationality with warm maternal compassion, through political ingenuity. "The trinity of the masochistic dream is summed up in the words: cold-maternal-severe, icy-sentimental-cruel." (Deleuze and Sacher-Masoch 1989, 51). Masochism does not suppress or brutalize feelings, but is rather a disavowal of quotidian sensuality in favor of a superior and more durable sensuality:

Under the cold remains a supersensual sentimentality buried under the ice and protected by fur; this sentimentality radiates in turn through the ice as the generative principle of new order, a specific wrath and a specific cruelty. The coldness is both protective milieu and medium, cocoon and vehicle: it protects supersensual sentimentality as inner life, and expresses it as external order, as wrath and severity (pp. 52).

This structure of thought and behavior is familiar. Just as masochism generates pleasure by practicing pain, Christianity deepens life by renouncing the things of this world. The tendency of masochism is to imitate Christ. To become, as Masoch wrote in a letter to his brother, "Man on the Cross, who knows no sexual love, no property, no fatherland, no cause, no work . . ." (as cited in CC 100). It was in this Deleuzian, Christian spirit that I first proposed my vision for a Neofeudal Technocommunism (Murphy 2018c). Neofeudal Technocommunism achieves collective freedom through a voluntary and delimited fascism over oneself (Murphy 2018b). It's a peaceful, sustainable model of communism based on historically unprecedented technologies for the production and maintenance of collective commitments. Namely, "smart contracts" (automated and irreversible contracts written with code on a blockchain) and increasingly ubiquitious passive monitoring hardware (i.e. the "Internet of Things"). Deleuze's insights from masochism will be especially useful in this regard, if I am correct that the contemporary Left is suffering from a short-circuiting of hyper-compassion (Murphy 2017b). The Left today is all maternal, all sentimental — no analytical coldness or icy honesty is permitted, even if a most severe glacier of gynocratic slave-morality nonetheless emerges as a "return of the repressed."

Deleuze helps us to see what is needed: creative pronomial assertion, a rectification of names not "against the Left," but from the Left and within the Left.[4] Applications of rationality icy enough to generate novel, autonomous, political orders, which are imperceptible and impenetrable to the representatives of status quo institutions. A divine

---

[4] As DC Miller told me, citing Confucius, conservatism is the "rectification of names" (Miller and Murphy 2019).

latency that equalizes distributions of warmth and resources through the ascetic renunciation of superficial warmth, fake equality, "pagan sensuality," and "sadistic sensuality." Indeed, the matter has now become surprisingly concrete in the form of the blockchain. As pure contractual immanence, cryptocurrencies running on distributed ledgers portend new reactionary-Left paths to autonomous communism. With the same paradoxical structure as masochism and Christianity, crypto portends an exit from capitalism, but only for those who voluntarily accelerate its capitalist logic. Deleuze would have been delighted.

Chapter Four

Bearing One's Cross

Deleuze was fond of saying that one should never object. In *Negotiations* (Deleuze 1995, 103), discussing detractors and haters, he says:

> *The objections people make, even the questions they pose, always come from safe ashore, and they're like lumps of mud flung at you to knock you down and stop you getting anywhere rather than any help: objections always come from lazy, mediocre people...*

In his collaborative interview-essay with Claire Parnet (2002), on the very first page he rejects the practice of "reflection." He adds:

> *Objections are even worse. Every time someone puts an objection to me, I want to say: 'OK, OK, let's go on to something else.' Objections have never contributed anything.*

A philosopher who refuses to object can hardly be a left-wing activist capable of *protesting*. For Deleuze, there is never any question of protesting injustice. He may think about, and articulate his thoughts about, various situations of social injustice. But Deleuze is resolutely Stoic and Christian in his understanding of injustice and suffering. Contemporary leftists would call Deleuze's ethics "victim blaming," but I would like to suggest that we consider them a post-activist portal to a non-resentful theory of collective liberation.

According to Deleuze, especially in his *Logic of Sense*, the injustices and misfortunes one suffers come before the self. "My wound existed before me: I was born to embody it" (Hallward 2006, 43).

Our sufferings, including material deprivations caused by more powerful individuals, are not *actualities* but *virtualities*. This is a crucial distinction throughout Deleuze's works, a distinction which we will revisit in a later chapter (*The Real, The Evolved, and the Traditional*). For now, it suffices to say the following. It is easy to see that actual facts are a relatively small component of the larger psychological and emotional ensemble constituting any "material deprivation" (e.g., the fact that someone has no money in their bank account is only one small portion of the much larger and often painful life experience called "poverty."). We know this because there is variation in the relationship between actual facts and psychological or emotional ensembles — for instance, the existence of people who are poor and joyous, and people who are rich and sad. Paraplegics handicapped by catastrophic accidents enjoy the same amount of happiness as lottery winners, on average, and lottery winners derive *less* happiness from everyday events (Brickman, Coates, and Janoff-Bulman 1978; Murphy 2018a).

Sufferings are not actual effects of material causes that can or should be corrected by some kind of organized operation. According to Deleuze, one's suffering is an *event,* and living through it is what endows one's life with a *destiny* (Hallward 2006, 43). Events are occurrences that are anomalous or surprising with respect to the pre-existing, normal, causal order. A life only becomes a life to the degree that one is faithful to the events that occur within it. Events, irreducible to causal predictors and structural factors, are the only things that make you you. And yet they are impersonal and accidental, so they will never lead you to the narcissistic spiritualism of believing that you must create your own worth *sui generis*. The event that is my wound does not *determine* my future, it is an immanent virtual occurrence that makes possible my future; it is only my task to live it. My life only emerges with its own consistency to the degree that I counter-actualize my wound. What Deleuze calls counter-actualization or virtualization means grasping the matter as an event, affirming the event as having occurred, and continuing to live in such a way that it is possible to love the event: *amor fati*. In this way, one becomes who one is, rather than resentfully trying always to be who one is not.[5]

---

[5] It follows that left-wing activists — in their obsession with the reduction of injustices and sufferings — unwittingly seek to rob the poor of their lives. So-called "Effective Altruism" is a higher-IQ version of the same logic.

Chapter Five

The Eternal Return

The concept of the eternal return in Nietzsche, and in Deleuze's reading of Nietzsche, is yet another concept with a confusing ideological valence. The eternal return is a notoriously vexing idea in Nietzsche's thought, and a wild variety of interpretations have been proposed. For my part, I read the eternal recurrence as an ethical device. The gist is that one should be capable of so absolutely affirming everything that has ever happened in one's life, that one is joyful at the thought of everything recurring infinitely. I won't try to adjudicate alternative interpretations here.

Deleuze analyzes the eternal recurrence as a "dice throw." There are two essential moments or stages in the dice throw (Deleuze 2006, 25–26). The first is the actual throw, and the second is when the dice falls back. To throw the dice, one must affirm *chance,* but when the dice settles, one must affirm *necessity.* The future unfolds as a series of dice throws. To affirm the eternal return is to affirm that life is but a series of dice throws — perpetual difference as a constant, the being of becoming.

The naïve way to read Deleuze here is to say that one should just be content with anything that happens. It's all random and futile, but to affirm anyway is a good exercise of the will. Take drugs recklessly, sleep around, don't take anything too seriously, just keep rolling the dice and affirm whatever happens.

In fact, the eternal return is a device for grounding commitments and living a meaningful, coherent, integrated life when God is dead and no trustworthy external supports can be found. The affirmation of the eternal return, correctly understood, generates a life of *austerity* and *discipline.* Whatever the dice throw gives me today, I must not only affirm today but tomorrow and the next day as well — I must affirm it eternally. The dice I throw tomorrow will produce different results, and I must affirm those results in addition to — not instead of — the results from today. To affirm life as a succession of dice throws implicitly requires the cognitive activity of *integrating* each dice throw.

A rigorous or integral accounting of one's life is not as stuffy as it sounds, for such integration requires a most profound kind of existential creativity. Indeed, rendering the results of tomorrow into consistency with the results of today is the essence of living freely. Revising the narrative of one's life, through conceptual amendments of the past as well as through additional performances and constructions in the future, while nonetheless maintaining fidelity to the unbroken thread of one's constitution and convictions… This is to write the most epic novel, paint the most epic canvas, and perform on the most epic stage, all at once. And yet, the enterprise revolves around a submission to the necessity of what is the case. Insofar as difference is the only constant of life, consistency or integrity is — ironically — the only variable, the only opportunity for freedom and creativity.

How will you make your life coherent? Only on a plane of immanence that you will construct yourself, Deleuze and Guattari tell us. ("You" refers to a machinic haeccaeity rather than a quotidian ego-subject, but nothing prevents us from retaining the same shorthand for our purposes.) Life is a creative project that can only be indexed to itself. By anchoring oneself to oneself over the dimension of time, one is forced to invent — forced to be free. Immanence and integrity are bedfellows.

To be clear, submission to what is the case does not imply resignation to whatever institutional status quo happens to reign. Quotidian institutional narratives are not "what is the case." Dominant narratives are almost by definition half-truths, insofar as they result from a large, diffuse, memetic selection process. When I speak of the submission to reality, I do not mean submission to what others believe to be reality. I mean submission to the data of reality — the data of one's life — including all the data on the pervasiveness of hypocrisy and deception in human affairs.

The social and political implications of the Eternal Return are therefore exactly the opposite of those drawn by the socially liberal nihilist. If you fall in love with your high school sweetheart, then get married! If you get married and it's not so great, then create a new narrative, new concepts, new practices — until it is great. If your spouse is not the person you thought they were when you married them, well, that's a roll of the dice and you must find a way to affirm it. Rather than see yourself as mistaken or aggrieved (common cop-outs cited by resentful or lazy people), your obligation to continue affirming necessity is one of the most powerful motive forces for creativity at the greatest scale possible: creatively revise the narrative of your life such that your marriage is no longer mistaken or you are no longer aggrieved. Perhaps this means creating a new concept of yourself, or a new concept of your spouse, or new behavioral or communicative practices, etc.

As Deleuze teaches in *Difference and Repetition* (Deleuze 1968), one's destiny plays out on many levels one cannot control, but one can at least *choose the levels.* Freedom is not control or power over what happens, it is our capacity to select how it happens to us:

42

However strong the incoherence or possible opposition between successive presents, we have the impression that each of them plays out 'the same life' at different levels. This is what we call destiny. Destiny never consists in step-by-step deterministic relations between presents which succeed one another according to the order of a represented time. Rather, it implies between successive presents non-localisable connections, actions at a distance, systems of replay, resonance and echoes, objective chances, signs, signals and roles which transcend spatial locations and temporal successions... This is why destiny accords so badly with determinism but so well with freedom: freedom lies in choosing the levels (pp. 83).

No matter how much you suffer, creativity means doing whatever needs to be done, within Necessity, to make life worth living. Necessity provides the fixed constraints along which the successive creations of your life will add up to a pure immanence and integral whole.

Dissolute people who betray commitments often invoke their "creativity" as an excuse — "How could I possibly contain my genius? How could I possibly contain my love?" But really people betray commitments because they are boring, unable to blaze new paths from difficult situations. The truly creative person will bear their cross no matter what, because they always find a way to blaze a new path.

A socially liberal nihilist who leaves their spouse to "be more creative" will never create anything substantial or enduring. Here is a person who rips up their canvas after one stroke. It is a resentful, boring, and morbid life that refuses to affirm any particular dice throw, simply because the universe failed to deliver one's fantastic expectations.

Chapter Six

Creativity Is Submission

To appreciate the based nature of Deleuze's project, it is helpful to contrast him with two of the other most famous post-structuralists. Derrida and Foucault essentially reject ontology, or the study of what exists (May 2005, 171). Both Derrida and Foucault primarily studied the obstacles blocking the way to a clear delineation of what exactly exists. For Derrida, language itself was the primary culprit, interminably deferring any ultimately coherent ontology. Following Heidegger's search for Being, Derrida found that Being consists in difference and play, not in a fixed foundation or base, but in the gaps between what is based. For Foucault, history or genealogy was his preferred analytical method for productively disrupting claims about what exists. Everything we see as base reality is, beneath the surface, contingent on micro-political processes, the origins of which always elude our grasp.

As Todd May points out, Deleuze's works are rather filled with ontology. "While Foucault and Derrida find ontology to be a threat to asking how one might live, Deleuze finds ontology to be the very route one must take in order to ask about it adequately," writes May (2005, 15). Whereas Foucault and Derrida linguistically and genealogically deconstruct the bases of our existence, Deleuze thinks liberation is only possible *through* a radically rigorous reckoning with base reality. It is true that he will find *difference* at the base, but this does not mean there is no base, as the naïve post-structuralist might infer. Although Delueze is more interested in becoming than being, he nonetheless insists on the *being of becoming.*

Deleuze thinks we should answer the question of how to live with a fidelity to the question of what really exists. If the death of God is a grand erosion of constraints, which leads to a paralysis of infinite choice and atomization, then Deleuze's solution via Nietzsche is a freely cultivated, self-imposed accountability to empirical reality. One reason why Deleuze is so confusing is that he talks so much about creativity, which has a connotation of openness (a personality correlate of left-wing ideology), but he believes creativity is only unlocked through a fidelity and accountability to ontology, which introduce connotations of constraint, conformism, and conservatism — at least compared to the literary ethos of "free play" one finds in someone like Derrida. For Deleuze, it is only a radical empirical basedness that makes possible true freedom and creativity. For the ultimate insight gained from a fidelity to reality is *how reality can be changed*, even if it cannot be changed any way one pleases. There is no access to the mechanisms whereby reality can be changed, wherever there is less than absolute fidelity to reality. Submission to a status quo reality reveals the paths to escape it, paths which exist objectively within it. Trying to create something new by ignoring or disobeying what really exists leads to a confused, incessant repetition of the same, a bewildered reproduction of the status quo no matter how much energy is applied. Look at all currently

47

existing left-wing activist organizations. Faithful obedience to that which is, *based submission*, is the condition *sine qua non* for exiting the status quo and creating something new.

Chapter Seven

A Fascist Mother, "The Best of Women"

Let us consider a psycho-biographical approach to understanding the ideological valence of Deleuze's thought. Political ideologies are known to be heritable — probably somewhere between 30% and 60% heritable (Hatemi et al. 2014) — so an author's family background must provide at least *some* clues about an author's ideological center of gravity. Most attitudes show a higher correlation with parental attitudes later in life, suggesting that individuals early in life experiment by deviating from their inherited center of gravity, before eventually settling their viewpoints somewhere closer to that center of gravity.

According to the joint biography of Deleuze and Guattari by Françoise Dosse (2011, 89), both of Deleuze's parents were ideologically conservative. Louis Deleuze was an engineer and small-business owner, before he closed-up shop to become an employee of a large aerospace engineering firm. Louis disliked the Popular Front, the left-wing coalition that came to power in 1936, instead favoring a relatively small paramilitary party known as the *Croix-de-Feu*. Originally consisting of World War I veterans, this faction was financially supported by French millionaire and benefactor of Mussolini, Françoise Coty. The party had a Catholic bent because the Catholic Church prohibited Catholics from supporting the monarchist Action Française. The *Croix-de-Feu* was essentially a French equivalent of the Nazi party in Germany and the National Fascist Party in Italy, although this tendency in France was much weaker (the party enjoyed only about a million members at the height of its popularity).

After the Popular Front came to power, Louis and his wife, Odette, were horrified by the empowerment of working-class people. The

Popular Front passed policies such as mandatory paid vacations for all workers. Gilles recalls Louis and Odette disgusted to find working-class people on the beaches of Deauville, where the Deleuze family vacationed in Normandy. "My mother, who was surely the best of women, said that it was impossible to go to a beach with people like that on it" (pp. 89). Notice that Deleuze does not disavow his mother or her disgust, prefacing his recollection with an emphatic endorsement of the woman.

To be fair, Gilles would report being delighted by the site of workers vacationing, in contrast to his parents. We might wonder about a grown man's capacity to remember objectively his emotions as an 11-year-old boy, but we should take his testament at face value. This expression of solidarity is not surprising, as Deleuze consistently expressed sympathy with the downtrodden throughout his life. What is surprising, however, is how Deleuze characterizes his parents' reactionary horror at the workers in Deauville.

Deleuze goes on to explain that his family name means "of the oak tree... A tree whose only concern, like that of my family, was to detach itself by escaping and taking the 'line of flight' of going completely adrift (pp. 89)." For anyone who knows Deleuze's work and sees Deleuze as a consistently left-wing thinker, it is baffling to find Deleuze describing his reactionary parents with concepts possessing a generally positive valence in his philosophy. In the Deleuzo-Guattarian philosophy especially, *escape* is a recurring object of desire and the *line of flight* a consistently endorsed, if dangerous, pathway of escape. They also spend a lot of time analyzing how lines of flight can go wrong, and fascism is arguably the chief failure mode they are most concerned to prevent. The *tree* has a negative valence in their work, as an old, simplistic, and oppressive image of thought. "Completely adrift" is the crux of the statement's critical force. Nonetheless, Deleuze is revealing a kind of Venn diagram in which reactionary fascism overlaps substantially with his own philosophy — even if the fascist vector is only a failure mode. Dosse passes over this surprising comment without discussion, no doubt because the academic consensus on Deleuze makes a fascist *problematique* unthinkable.

Deleuze never joined the Resistance during the Nazi occupation of France, though he was only 18 at the time of his final year in high school. Yet neither did he enlist in the war, when he could have (Dosse 2011, 92). I am not suggesting he liked the Nazis; he certainly did not, at all. I am only pointing out that he did not wish to fight them, as the antifascist LARPers of today would seem to require.

Chapter Eight

From Christ to the Bourgeoisie

Deleuze's ideological complexity is already apparent in one of his first serious essays. *From Christ to the Bourgeoisie* (Deleuze 1946) is typically understood to be anti-Christ and anti-capitalist. Yet this interpretation seems plainly incorrect, as far as I can tell. Consider first that the essay is dedicated to a one Marie-Magdeleine Davey. First of all, Davey was known for frequenting the salons of Marcel Moret, a leftist Catholic (an ideological combination much more common in Deleuze's context than we observe anywhere in the West today). Davey was herself a fervent spiritualist who earned a degree in theology from the Paris Catholic Institute and later a doctorate in theology (Dosse 2011, 91). She enjoyed an accomplished career translating many works of twelfth-century French Catholics. Deleuze first met Davy in 1943, at a castle called La Fortrelle, where she hosted a seminar attended mostly by intellectuals with Christian and mystical tendencies (Wiel 2010).

Given the dedication to Marie-Magdeleine Davy, it is unthinkable that Deleuze would have understood his essay as straightforwardly anti-Christian. Deleuze was a young man and Davy was an impressive, accomplished figure who played an important brokering role in the intellectual milieu that Deleuze respected. I am not suggesting that Deleuze compromised the content of his ideas to impress Davy, but rather that if his intentions were simply anti-Christian he would not have dedicated it to Davy.

In the words of Raymond van de Wiel, who translated the essay into English, "While the article appears to criticize religion, some arguments Deleuze uses to articulate this criticism seem to be influenced by the Christian mysticism that had been widely embraced by French intellectuals, from around 1910 until, roughly, the end of the 1940s" (Wiel 2010). The essay's partial anti-Christian connotations are only directed at a particular conception of Christianity popular at the time, the neo-Thomism associated with Jacques Maritain. Maritain is no longer a household name, but he was huge at the time. Confusingly, though we today would think of Catholic social teachings as conservative relative to triumphant social liberalism in the West, Maritain represented a humanistic liberalization of Christianity in his day. In short, to the degree this essay is anti-Christian, it is opposed to the neo-Thomist *liberalization* of Christianity.

In one sense, "interiority" has a negative valence. Almost always, the "outside" is where Deleuze wants to look, whereas interiority is a morbid tendency to be avoided. But in this essay, he cites lamentably the popular impression that Spirit has been exhausted, adding that, "What we want to say is that today many people no longer believe in interior life." So he does acknowledge there is a problem to be solved here. What we find through a close reading of this essay is that, from the beginning of his career, Deleuze is not dismissing the catastrophe of inner experience besetting modern man. He believes that we have become attached to a sick conception of interiority, not that Spirit, inner experience, or interiority as such are trivial or contemptible concerns. Quite the contrary, Deleuze will be obsessed with essentially private, anti-social, mental experiences, even if he will be equally interested in how such experiences do or do not connect with others' experiences.

Deleuze's criticism of liberal-humanist Christianity is that Christ is understood as bringing the "good news" of an Outside, but ultimately this Outside is itself interiority. Liberal-humanist Christianity only cares about human nature: reduce sin, pray, turn the other cheek, etc. This version of Christianity "has not come to save the world, [but has come] to save us from the world." Deleuze is calling for a true Christianity, which indeed comes to save the world.

The Christianity Deleuze is implicitly endorsing in this essay is the Christianity favored by Davy (and the mystics she studied, such as St. Thierry). Roughly, whereas the Thomist tradition tends to value intellect over desire/love, what is sometimes called the "affectivist" mystic tradition values desire/love over intellect. As van de Wiel notes, Deleuze's argument in this essay — one that also reappears much later in *What is Philosophy?* (Deleuze and Guattari 1994) — recapitulates the arguments advanced by an anonymous 14th century mystic in a manuscript called *The Cloud of Unknowing*. As I am not much of a medievalist, I can do no better than quote van de Wiel's competent summary of the *Cloud* logic:

> *The Cloud-author distinguishes between a false 'image' of interiority and true interiority. The false image of interiority comes to life when one tries to describe spiritual life, as the intellectual tradition does, in terms of spatial metaphors of 'above' and 'below', and 'within' and 'without'. The Cloud author then warns that these words can easily be misinterpreted. Those who conclude on the basis of these images that one should leave behind all historical and bodily aspects of life and translate interiority simply into mental acts, are mistaken, he holds, and become trapped in a vicious circle. They base their view of interiority on the distinction between interiority and*

exteriority, which depends on intellectual imaginative opposition which, one could say, can only be thought from the outside. But this is not true wisdom; in fact it is madness, says the Cloud author, it is a fantasy, it is "against nature". They have not truly grasped interiority. Paradoxically, this true interiority does not know of 'inner' and 'outer', does not distinguish between 'bodily' and 'ghostly'; "Our inner man calleth it All".

This logic reappears in *What is Philosophy?* as the basis for what Deleuze and Guattari refer to as immanence. When Deleuze rejects the morbid modern cult of interiority, he is not prioritizing its opposite, some grand and vital exterior on the outside of the interior. It is our constant return to this distinction itself — this "intellectual imaginative opposition" in the words of the *Cloud* — that is the pathology. Rather, Deleuze's whole career champions *true interiority*, which has no need for any exterior at all. It doesn't begin with any awareness of, or reference to, an exterior from which it enjoys its self-consciousness as interior. Neither does it come around to some exterior later, for it is so interior there is no exterior anywhere to be found. Confusingly, Deleuze and Guattari name this radical interiority the Outside. Deleuze's radical interiority — as we have seen, a Catholic interiority — is a militant, intuitive, non-intellectual relationship with an infinitely distant God. The Outside is "more distant than any external world because it is an inside deeper than any internal world: it is immanence (Deleuze and Guattari 1994, 59)."

One should be clear that this is not a dialectic. It is not as if one accesses true interiority through the Outside, which at a certain point of development becomes interior. Similarly, one does not get Outside by a development of interiority, which becomes its opposite. Rather, there exists an Outside, infinite and beyond our reach, and we are its continuous and uninterrupted unfolding. We are composed of the same substance, but in a finite form. God is the traditional name for this Outside force or ultimate agency we only *know* through our distance from it, and which we nonetheless *embody* virtually in all that we do.

The political implications are striking. We have shown that it is ludicrous to see Deleuze as anti-Christian, but what can we say about his purported anti-capitalism? With respect to Christianity, we have shown that his enemy is not Christianity but a false distinction at the heart of morbid, modernized, liberalized Christianity. Namely, the intellectualized opposition of interiority/exteriority, or spirit/nature. With respect to capitalism, his perspective is analogous. Just as his implicit "anti-Christian" target in this essay is Maritain, his implicit anti-capitalist target is Jean-Paul Sartre. Sartre was the epitome of a Marxist, activist intellectual, who believed fervently in workers organizing for Communist revolution. Deleuze is not so much attacking the bourgeoisie, as he is attacking what is morbid about the bourgeoisie (and Sartre's attitude).

Subtweeting Sartre's *Critique of Dialectical Reason*, Deleuze rehearses the notion that some Leader will eventually reveal to workers a new possible world, say, where they no longer work for their bosses (Deleuze 1946). Deleuze suggests that such Sartrean anti-capitalism is morbid for the same reason that Maritain's liberal Christian humanism is morbid. The workers would not be released into the Outside of their freedom, but yet another exterior (relative to an interior): The workers will now be slaves to whoever or whatever represents the Leader function, whether it's Josef Stalin or some local social-justice cadre. One could say that in the work of Sartre, the false distinction analogous to humanist Christianity's nature/spirit might be the distinction between inert complicity with capitalist exploitation and commitment to justice (inertia/ activism, for short). Just as the false oppositions of liberal Christianity lead to a fake kind of salvation, the false oppositions of Sartrean anti-capitalism lead to a fake kind of liberation: merely "a commitment to commitment."

It is now possible to infer the outlines of Deleuze's unique theological and ideological position. First, Deleuze affirmed a traditional Catholic fidelity to God in the only way possible given his context of liberal-modernizing Christianity: God is so far outside modern, morbid human intellection, precisely because God is so *right here* that we cannot believe it. And he affirmed a commitment to revolutionary, collective liberation in the only way possible given the context of a Stalinesque Communist Left. The theological and political solution, in both cases, is the realization that there has never been a problem. This is the "good news" of Christ and the key to a non-suicidal movement of collective liberation. The perception of a problem that then calls forth morbid, resentful responses is only the result of needless and mistaken distinctions generated by morbid, modern intellection. To say that there is no problem is not to say that there is nothing to do. Quite the contrary, to realize there is no problem is precisely what makes it possible to *create,* which is the Deleuzian key to both a non-morbid Christian ethics and a non-resentful political activism.

Chapter Nine

Deleuzo-Petersonianism

Despite the extraordinary rise to fame of Canadian
psychologist Jordan Peterson, most people still
know nothing about his scholarly contributions to
political psychology research. And most fans of
Jordan Peterson know nothing about the better
figures of late twentieth-century Continental
Philosophy, not least because of Peterson's broad
condemnations of "postmodern neo-Marxism." It's
no wonder that people make fun of my claim that
there's a lot of common ground between Jordan
Peterson and Gilles Deleuze. There is currently no
audience for this common ground, because the fans
of each figure generally dislike the other figure. As
if this book is not already idiosyncratic enough, the
thoughts that follow are therefore especially

untimely, solitary — written from a literal desert, as it happens. But to use the language of Deleuze and Guattari, my solitude is "a populous solitude, like the desert itself, a solitude already intertwined with a people to come, one that invokes and awaits that people, existing only through it, though it is not yet here" (Deleuze and Guattari 1987, 377). That's you, dear reader…

If there exists a true claim for which no audience yet exists, develop the claim until you produce its audience. Stage one is laughter, stage two is the creation of a new people (who come curious about the laughter but become the subject of the truth in development). This is four-dimensional memetic warfare. Deleuze and Guattari first discovered this mechanism through the lives of artistic figures such as Franz Kafka. Not properly Jewish, German, or Austro-Hungarian, Kafka's "people" were missing and his literature sought to produce them (Deleuze and Guattari 1986). Jordan Peterson executed this teaching of Deleuze and Guattari with unprecedented success. For years, he wrote books and recorded videos on the fringes of academic psychology, despite there existing no constituency for them. Only later, as his videos became popular among frustrated young men, did those videos start to produce the people they were made for, at a scale and velocity unprecedented for a random, mild-mannered academic. Of course, I am executing the same procedure, and as we continue to lay bare the source-code for such procedures, eventually everyone will be able to produce their own people (or join someone else's people).

Latent Inhibition

Between 2000 and 2005, Jordan Peterson and various co-authors published a series of articles relating to the psychological concept known as "latent inhibition" (Peterson and Carson 2000; Peterson, Smith, and Carson 2002). With only a little stretching, we will interpret their framework and findings as an empirical-psychological version of the Deleuzian viewpoint on the nature of creativity and philosophical innovation. We'll begin with Deleuze and circle back to Peterson's research on latent inhibition.

For Deleuze, one of the most important questions, a question that runs throughout his oeuvre, is: How is novelty possible? As the Stanford Encylopedia of Philosophy puts it in their entry on Deleuze, "the aim of philosophy is not to rediscover the eternal or the universal, but to find the singular conditions under which something new is produced (Smith and Protevi 2018)." Deleuze was known for his interest in the arts, especially literature and film, because the arts offer models for how creativity works. For instance, cinema enables a modern view of movement, which is "capable of thinking the production of the new (Deleuze 1986)." One of the reasons that Deleuze and Guattari wrote a lot about schizophrenia is that schizophrenics dramatize a radical openness to novelty. Deleuze and Guattari were also famous for their interest in animal life, and their use of examples from the animal kingdom to develop their political ethics. Curiously, they always insisted that their animal models were not metaphorical but literal. They spoke of animal-becomings in humans, and they meant it.

Jordan Peterson was long interested in the adjacent question of why some people are more creative than others. In fact, his empirical research explicitly addresses the relation between creativity and schizophrenia. He, too, often draws on animal models (though many psychologists do).

In a 2002 article of particular interest to us, Peterson and co-authors study the psychological phenomenon known as Latent Inhibition (Peterson, Smith, and Carson 2002). Latent Inhibition is a technical term for the "pre-conscious gating mechanism that allows animals with complex nervous systems to ignore stimuli previously experienced as irrelevant" (pp. 1138). Low levels of Latent Inhibition, they note, have been associated with schizophrenia. The article goes on to test some hypotheses about the relationship between Latent Inhibition, personality traits, and creativity. They are essentially testing psychological and neurobiological mechanisms consistent with certain Deleuzian propositions.

One could go deeper into this literature, and possibly extricate a much larger scientific basis for a variety of Deleuze's philosophical intuitions. This would require another book. For now, the following stylized summary should suffice.

Deleuze was interested in explaining how individuals and groups can sense and maneuver around their particular thresholds of Latent Inhibition. Although it's a pre-conscious gating mechanism, it has certain recurring behavioral and perceptual correlates, which can be identified and used to reverse engineer the workings of the Latent Inhibition threshold. The Latent Inhibition threshold is dangerous, because if it's too low you go mad but if it's too high you're boring at best and fascist at worst. The trick is to understand where it is, how it can be manipulated, and how to navigate it.

It is not implausible that Peterson and Deleuze even shared some substantive motivations. At the root of both projects is the question of how to generate and sustain creative vitality without falling into the traps of fascism. Peterson has said many times that one of his abiding motivations has been to understand how totalitarian violence becomes possible, while Foucault said of Deleuze's co-authored book *Anti-Oedipus* (Deleuze and Guattari 1983) that it was an introduction or manual to the non-fascist life. Far from glorifying schizophrenia, Deleuze wanted to know how we could be more creative without falling into the trap dramatized by schizophrenics. With this brief sojourn through some work by Jordan Peterson, we access yet another window into the most based dimensions of Deleuze's radical philosophical project.

Against Maximum Deterritorialization

Jordan Peterson is known for his conservative fears of radical-left excess — that young "social justice warriors" roaming college campuses might soon be erecting national gulags. Although they are not known for it, Deleuze and Guattari are equally concerned about the excesses of naïve radical leftism. Given the preceding analysis of a substantial theoretical overlap between Deleuze and Peterson, it is plausible that they all feared radical Left excesses for the same basic reasons.

According to Peterson and Carson (2000), schizophrenia is generated in part by a combination of high Openness and low Intelligence. Creativity, on the other hand, is generated in part by the combination of high Openness and high Intelligence. In short, if your Latent Inhibition is low so that your "gate" allows in a lot of affectively charged information, you are likely to become either creative or insane — depending on your level of intelligence.

Deleuze obviously had no access to these scientific literatures, which would only be developed later. However, his empirical intuitions are uncannily prescient and consistent with Peterson's model, although Deleuze and Guattari are more interested in extrapolating the political implications. Deleuze and Guattari observe that it is the most radically creative or "deterritorializing" individuals and groups who unleash the flows most likely to backlash or "reterritorialize" pathologically. They do not explicitly refer to intelligence as a moderating variable, but this is no wonder given their political context and how much intelligence research was still yet to come. Nonetheless, Deleuze and Guattari implicitly invoke intelligence as a moderating variable in their socio-political models. For instance, consider the passage below, in which they distinguish between the creativity of merchants and the dependency of the bureaucrats and peasants.

> *It is precisely the most deterritorialized flow, under the first aspect, that always brings about the accumulation or conjunction of the processes, determines the overcoding, and serves as the basis for reterritorialization under the second aspect (we have already encountered a theorem according to which it is always on the most deterritorialized element that reterritorialization takes place). For example, the merchant bourgeoisie of the cities conjugated or capitalized a domain of knowledge, a technology, assemblages and circuits into whose dependency the nobility, Church, artisans, and even peasants would enter. It is precisely because the bourgeoisie was a cutting edge of deterritorialization, a veritable particle accelerator, that it also performed an overall reterritorialization (1987, 220–21).*

When we recall that in Deleuze's vocabulary, "dependency" is a word he associates with schizophrenics (see the chapter, *HBDeleuze*), we are able to translate this dense passage into plain English. The liberating creativity of the most intelligent merchants unleashed so many novel flows, that it made all the bureaucrats and peasants relatively more schizophrenic. The oppressive and pathological political formations that arose in the wake of these early-modern merchants were a result of the less intelligent classes seeking to police the flows that threatened to drown them. The parallels between Deleuze and Peterson come full circle today, as the "social justice warriors" fomenting distributed authoritarian-censorship are perhaps individuals insufficiently intelligent to process and creatively maneuver all the new flows unleashed by accelerating digital intensification. Deleuze and Peterson are both trying to understand and promote the conditions for creative, intelligent, negentropy production (art, science, entrepreneurship, etc.). They are also trying to understand and discourage — with a shared reactionary horror — the conditions that make the less intelligent erect resentful and harmful political formations, whether those be early-modern mercantilist states, bureaucracies, "safe spaces," or gulags.

Chapter Ten

$\mathcal{HB}\,\mathcal{D}eleuze$

Human biodiversity (HBD) is the idea that average differences in various traits can be observed across human populations, due to the existence of different evolutionary selection pressures in different times and places. To leftists today, the concept of HBD is nothing more or less than old-fashioned, pseudo-scientific racism. It is certainly true that, to some white nationalists and internet trolls, the phrase "human biodiversity" can function as a technically innocent and scientistic slogan for some nasty ideas and intentions. Nonetheless, for most normal people and many professional researchers, there is a certain obvious, harmless, and incontrovertible reality beneath the HBD idea: Some people are tall, some people are short, etc. And most people today will affirm the theory of evolution as the best available explanation for all the diversity of living organisms. So who cares?

HBD has become a uniquely polarizing lightning rod today because it suggests there may be real, average differences in traits *across races.* For the same reason some human populations evolve to have white skin, and others evolve to have black or brown skin, some populations evolve to have more or less of various attitudinal and behavioral traits as well.

I'm not a specialist in this area, and this book is not about the HBD debate, so I won't opine needlessly. What's most important is that the HBD idea — whether true or false — is *prohibited* within most currently existing institutionalized status games. To cite only the most recent example, intelligence researcher Noah Carl was recently dismissed from his post at the University of Cambridge because of a petition associating his relatively run-of-the-mill psychology research with an HBD framing (Carl 2019). This cultural sensitivity goes back all the way to Darwin's time, but our era's generalized prohibition on HBD goes back at least to the middle of the 1970s. E.O Wilson's *Sociobiology* (1975) was probably the first time, in the post-war period, that a major scholarly work arguing in favor of HBD produced a significant, public backlash. More memorable to contemporary readers might be the case of Charles Murray, whose co-authored book *The Bell Curve* (1996) is explicitly classified as pseudo-scientific racist anathema in most graduate humanities programs today.

The reason for this historical interlude back to 1975 is that Deleuze's first explicitly political book was co-authored with Félix Guattari in 1972. The second, also co-authored with Guattari, was written in 1980. *Anti-Oedipus* and *A Thousand Plateaus* sandwich all the controversies and protests around sociobiology that raged in the 1970s. My argument will not be that the sociobiology debates were a subtext of Deleuze's work with Guattari. My point is only to establish that, as the widespread riots of the late 1960s had already brought the issue into many living rooms, extreme political sensitivity to race talk was already a live wire in the 1970s.

It is therefore stunning to read Deleuze and Guattari's many references to traits being unequally distributed across individuals and groups, including racial groups. Understanding the political sensitivity of the 1970s now helps us to explain a long-standing puzzle that has vexed so many: Why did Deleuze and Guattari seem to write with such purposeful obscurity? It seems very likely that a vaguely Straussian technique is at work, in which Deleuze and Guattari (or perhaps just Deleuze) purposely develop a prohibitively idiosyncratic language in order to smuggle in certain ideas then prohibited by the political Left. They could not be seen as developing an HBD-consistent political theory without becoming anathema in left-wing milieus (high-status French intellectual life in general was a left-wing milieu). But they could if they remained *unclear,* at least to the majority of their readers — the dumb majority who will claim to love anything fashionable, even if they don't understand it.

We are now in a position to catalogue some of Deleuze and Guattari's most emphatically "problematic" beliefs.

First of all, Deleuze in particular was always surprisingly frank about his preference for the strong over the weak. His pro-hierarchical attitude comes out most clearly, and perhaps least surprisingly, in his Nietzsche book (Deleuze 2006). Writing fondly of Nietzsche's unabashed aristocracism, Deleuze says:

> *One of the finest remarks in* The Will to Power *is: "The strong always have to be defended against the weak" (VP I 395).*

Even Deleuze's biographer, Dosse, acknowledges Deleuze's taste for the strong over the weak. It is unfortunate that Dosse simply skips over in silence this reactionary affirmation at odds with his supposedly left-wing philosopher. Note in particular the implicit reference to an evolutionary-psychological model (Dosse 2011, 131):

> *Arguing against the notion that everything that is produced returns in cyclical movements, Deleuze sees the eternal return as the result of a selection of the strong and an elimination of the weak. "It makes of will something whole. The thought of the eternal return eliminates from will everything which falls outside the eternal return, it makes of*

will a creation, it carries out the equation 'to will = to create.'"

Deleuze wants to purify the will, to remove from it all that is weak, through a brutal and eternally recurring process of Darwinian selection. Deleuzian creativity is not fun and games for old ladies and kids: rather it is only for the strong, who have the will to mercilessly filter their own thoughts down to the eternal. This is no walk in the park, folks.

While we're talking about purity, Deleuze and Guattari even have the nerve to call for a *purification of race* (1987, 98).

> *To be a bastard, a half-breed, but through a purification of race. That is when style becomes a language. That is when language becomes intensive, a pure continuum of values and intensities. That is when all of language becomes secret, yet has nothing to hide, as opposed to when one carves out a secret subsystem within language.*

Of course, I am not submitting that Deleuze and Guattari are closeted white supremacists. I am submitting that, in their work, we observe an emphatic refusal of Left moralism on race talk, a Left moralism which was already present in the

79

1970s and is now at a fever pitch in 2019. They are not racists — not at all — but rather *race-accelerationists*: The liberation of oppressed races will not be won through "anti-racism," which has resentment built into its very concept, but through a kind of excessive elaboration of races. Because the concept of race is the morbid fixation of an uncreative identity, purifying it means exposing it to the Nietzschean "eternal recurrence," which means, as we have seen, Darwinian selection. Purification of race does not mean harboring but exhausting it, shedding all that is rotten within it. Purifying means filtering until all that is left is a real kernel, a real core. And the real core of race ultimately has little to do with race, but rather the continuous variation of creativity, previously overcoded by race: this is why the result is to become a bastard, to finally have done with race, in favor of a positive, forward march on unique lines of flight. Language here "becomes secret" not because one has carved out some obscure code, but only because one has entered onto a unique, individual, intuitive perspective beyond or beneath status quo social expectations and conventional intellection. One hides nothing, and yet one is now endowed with a secret language, simply because one has entered into genuine creativity (LaFinta 2004).

If you walk into a left-wing activism meeting today talking about *any* kind of purity, you'll be met with cold glares at best. If you walk in talking about a purification of the will, forget about it! If you walk in talking about a purification of race, unless you're black or brown, well, just stick a fork in you because you are *done*! But Deleuze and Guattari pull it off...

Deleuze was also never shy about his contempt and disgust toward marginalized people (they called them "marginals" back then). Let us note, by the way, that disgust-sensitivity is a robust correlate of political conservatism (Inbar, Pizarro, and Bloom 2009). Speaking about the mentally ill in particular, Deleuze says in his interview-essay with Claire Parnet (Deleuze and Parnet 2002, 139):

> *Schizophrenia is the descent of a molecular process into a black hole. Marginals have always inspired fear in us, and a slight horror. They are not clandestine enough. (NOTE: In any case, they scare me... It is a*

disaster when they slip into a black hole from which they no longer utter anything but the micro-fascist speech of their dependency and their giddiness: 'We are the avant-garde', 'We are the marginals.'... DG).

The parenthetical caveat distinguishing Deleuze's exclusive ownership of this remark is likely there because Claire Parnet was a career journalist. One can hear her saying, "Um, Gilles…" and Deleuze saying, "OK, OK, the Based Philosopher will clarify and sign his own name to this." I draw attention to this minor wrinkle because it is another data point showing that Deleuze would have been perfectly conscious of the culture wars beginning to intensify at this time. The conflict between "social justice warriors" and real intellectuals is not peculiar to our time.

Chapter Eleven

Becoming Imperceptible

Deleuze and Guattari repeatedly stress the importance of *becoming imperceptible*, but the idea remains poorly understood.

When this phrase gets tossed around today, especially on the internet, it's often to glorify obscurity. Deleuze and Guattari are used to justify a certain kind of hiding. Consider, for instance, the number of anonymous Twitter accounts emitting Deleuzian takes with esoteric usernames and illegible digital avatars. I take no issue with such stylistic preferences, and there are often good reasons for them, but they don't follow from a Deleuzo-Guattarian politics of imperceptibility. In fact, as I'll explain below, Deleuze and Guattari are clear that a characteristic of becoming imperceptible is *having no need for masks* and *nothing to hide.* This is only one example of how the notion of becoming imperceptible is widely misunderstood.

More importantly, though, I should begin with why becoming imperceptible is such an important and attractive idea. Not just for Deleuze and Guattari, or even for their audience, but for everyone. For Deleuze and Guattari, becoming imperceptible names the peak experience of an agent in a process of liberation. It is the pinnacle stage of escape or *releasement* (Murphy and Niederhauser 2019) from everything that seems so good at dominating, confusing, and capturing our potential energy and capacities.[6]

These forces of domination are called by many names in the Deleuzo-Guattarian register: the *molar*, the *rigid segments*, the *strata*, etc., among others. One of the reasons why the models of Deleuze and Guattari are so difficult to understand

---

[6] On Heidegger's *releasement* (*gelassenheit*) and its connections to Deleuzian escape, see my course with Johannes Niederhauser at theotherlifenow.com/deleuze-vs-heidegger.

is that they seek to pinpoint the operation of these forces at a very fine resolution, but in the most general and abstract terms they can find - to capture a lot of conditional variances without getting lost in the weeds, remaining maximally applicable to diverse situations. The cost, of course, is an infamous cornucopia of unwieldy terms.

For shorthand, I prefer to call these various mechanisms of domination, as a set, *the institutions*. Everywhere we look today, we see perverse institutions, often ancient institutions in path-dependent zombie modes; these institutions are often characterized by obvious and extreme deceptions, internal and external; they often malfunction regularly in predictable ways, and in ways that are easily solvable, but the solutions are often structurally prohibited by the very functioning of the institutions at some higher level.

Schools, criminal justice systems, pathological families, corporations, universities, media, etc.: all of these institutions are molar aggregates that require our participation and capture our possibilities, in ways that appear increasingly insane and undesirable to increasing numbers of people (if for extremely different reasons, or rather reasons stated in extremely different languages). For instance, a leftist may say the primary institutional culprits are labor markets and "institutionalized" racism and so on, whereas conservatives may point to the university, labor unions, etc. One of the reasons for the bizarre vocabulary of Deleuze and Guattari is, I believe, to sidestep these ideologically conditional forking paths — not in some wish to be bipartisan but simply because these are institutionally captured pathways which foreclose access to the very problem we would like to solve.

At stake here is figuring out how to live under the weight of increasingly complex institutions that are increasingly good at reproducing themselves — to understand them not just philosophically but empirically — in order that we may outsmart them and maneuver with increasingly greater freedom. Something like this is what I mean when I use the term "liberation." In my own view, the scientifically valid identification of the mechanisms of liberation, and their diffusion throughout a culture, is all that "revolutionary politics" could ever mean. And while Deleuze and Guattari are somewhat coy about their ultimate stances on what a successful revolutionary politics would look like, I remain convinced that their theoretical project is essentially to map and model the mechanisms of what I would call liberation. In any event, no matter what register one might prefer today, almost everybody is interested in some kind of escape, exit, or liberation from some kind of opaque institutional pathology.

According to Deleuze and Guattari, becoming imperceptible is the crucial final stage of any genuine escape path. Not final in the sense that everything is completed once and for all, but final in the sense that it's the zenith of a particular, repeatable mechanism — the famous "line of flight." If they are correct, then everybody should be interested in what it means to become imperceptible. Indeed, if you wish to live at all today, rather than merely survive, increasingly you *must* become imperceptible.

Being Perceived Means Being Manipulated

For obvious reasons, we have strong inclinations to be understood by others. There is a problem here because, to the degree we wish to be perceptible to others, we are conditioning our own expressions on contingent social and political variables. In an ideal community, this might not be a problem. If technological or other contextual variables veer off in a way that biases and malforms popular perceptions, then thinking and speaking to be perceptible can easily lock one into a life of inescapable confusion, suffering, and reproduction of precisely what one despises. This is the problem of perceptibility, in a nutshell.

Note that perception refers to sense data. Perceptibility therefore has pre-conscious connotations. You might think of perception as kind of like "understanding," but the latter is misleading because it connotes conscious intellection. It's worth clarifying this point because the problem here is not the prospect of being correctly understood intellectually. We will seek to be understood, but only by those who can understand. Seeking to be perceptible means catering to the initial and cheapest pieces of others' psychological and behavioral equipment.

To be perceptible means that institutions, and their human trustees, know how to manipulate you. Being perceptible means you are easily pigeonholed, and what's worse is that often you are correctly pigeonholed. If you optimize for how you are perceived, and especially if you build a life on how you are perceived (i.e., anyone who's income is based on status in an institutional hierarchy), then your thoughts, words, and actions are easily controlled by anyone above you in the institutional hierarchy. For by definition their edicts have greater influence on the perceptions of everyone attuned to the hierarchy than anything you might say or do, thus pleasing one's status-superiors is a necessity for those who wish to be perceived well. This matter is greatly complicated in contexts of institutional breakdown and fragmentation, as we are currently observing, so we will need to treat the matter in greater detail later; but for now, most of us are still maneuvering lives overwhelmingly characterized by the inertia of mass institutions, so even if institutions break down rapidly over the course of the next few generations, the general lessons here will suffice for most people for quite some time.

Being Perceived Means Being Highjacked

Another problem with being perceptible is easy to understand in our current digital context. It is a problem we might summarize as the motivational problem. Being perceived triggers dopamine, and dopamine hits train you to do more of whatever got you the dopamine. The more your motivation relies on dopamine via perceivability, the more surely you are not creating original and longer-term projects, because such projects require long periods of zero perceivability. When Deleuze and Guatarri say "bring something incomprehensible into the world (1987, 378)," this is what they are saying. They're not saying that any old nonsense should be brought into the world, or that ideas or artworks should be impenetrable by design. Deleuze and Guattari are saying that nothing worth thinking, saying, or making will pre-fit the perceptual schemas of others, in advance. All worthy creative projects are incomprehensible at first, when they are brought into the world. Any project that is immediately comprehensible is the product of someone opportunistically filling currently existing schemas of perception. That is the opposite of creation, that type of work is taking orders from arbitrary social opinion dynamics (guess where those opinions are most likely to come from, guess the higher function those opinions are most likely to serve). They are not railing against clear communication or transparent self-presentation; they are railing against anyone who creates in order to be valued from within already existing schemas of perception. Perfectly normal communication and self-presentation can totally scramble perceptions, and the most esoteric, anonymous, scrambled communications can be slavishly pre-fit to pre-existing perceptions.

If one is not creating on the fuel provided by immediate recognition, how is the work of creation motivated in the period of zero perceivability? To create anything other than reproductions of the status quo requires a different kind of motivational system. Lo and behold, Deleuze and Guattari offer one, which at every point is contrasted to capture by perceivability. They advise one to rather construct a plane of immanence (a "DGAF" gesture of creative violence, which is intrinsically self-rewarding) and then to work on it as a labor of love. "The secret always has to do with love (1987, 97)". But this is no cliché; while many of their analyses are about the mechanisms of domination, many others are dedicated to modeling in exquisite detail what the labor of love involves, and how to do it. If you can't access such a state, it is because you are captured, if not by perceptibility then by some other trap ("Is it good? Is it worth it?" Questions that usually veil a "What will people think?"). Thus, becoming imperceptible is about constituting a different kind of project, on a different motivational system - a system of immanent, intrinsically self-motivating creative productivity, rather than a mediated, extrinsic, alienated toil the satisfaction of which is always out of reach.

To make an irresistible reference back to the Twitter Deleuzians with which we began, it is some vindication of my contention here that the digital masks of these individuals do not seem to help in the slightest with this problem of capture by perceivability. For many of these people are prolific with short bursts of creative possibility, so long as they receive a perceptual payment of dopamine; but very rarely can these individuals bring such creative bursts to the constitution of a plane of immanence. This is because, as we will see, the mask is the face.

So the problem of being perceived is capture, susceptibility to manipulation, and losing the ability to create and execute works of substance.

Chapter Twelve

Accelerate the Process

.

If one had to boil down Deleuze's economic ideology — his essential position toward capitalism and markets — one would have to say that he is a market anarchist.[7] He clearly qualifies as what we would now call an accelerationist, but we'll discuss that in a moment. Market anarchists tend to be coded as left-wing insofar as they see capital and capitalism with a negative valence, but they are coded as right-wing insofar as they see markets with a positive valence. Capital, monopoly, and capitalism are vectors of oppression, but markets and entrepreneurship are vectors of liberation.

---

[7] I thank Edmund Berger for a lengthy conversation on this point. See Berger (2017), Holland (2011), and Land (1993).

Market anarchists believe markets are anti-capitalist, whereas the conventional view is to lump capital and markets into one big idea of capitalism.

Deleuze and Guattari were likely introduced to this perspective through Fernand Braudel, a historical sociologist who specialized in the study of early modern capitalism at ground level. Braudel found that capitalism emerges as an "anti-market," a result of agents adopting various non-entrepreneurial, rent-seeking tactics (Braudel 1982, 230). Today, political scientists know that disagreement over "government intervention in the market" is the primary political cleavage (the dimension of debate that best predicts individuals' positions on other issues). But according to Braudel, government intervention to balance the market was precisely what produced capitalism as we know it (i.e., all the anti-social tendencies we today attribute incorrectly to markets as such).

Throughout the two volumes of *Capitalism and Schizophrenia,* Deleuze and Guattari rely heavily on the distinction between *deterritorialization* and *reterritorialization.* Deterritorialization generally has a positive valence (though it's not so simple), connoting joy, creativity, and liberation. Reterritorialization generally has a negative valence (though it's not so simple), connoting sadness, inertia, and conservatism. The simplest way to understand these unwieldy terms is through the lens of market anarchism. Markets and entrepreneurs deterritorialize: the price mechanism distributes information about where, when, and how to create new projects of social value, and entrepreneurs overthrow oppressive institutions and undercut dominant monopolies in order to do so. Capitalism is what we call the reterritorialization of markets: successful entrepreneurs buy political power or become statesmen, incompetent entrepreneurs who lose in the market use democratic tactics to lobby for privileges and protections, etc.

It is in this light that we can now understand the famous accelerationist passage in the first volume of Deleuze and Guattari's joint work. After discussing some problems with Marxism, they ask:

So what is the solution? Which is the revolutionary path?… To withdraw from the world market, as Samir Amin advises Third World countries to do, in a curious revival of the fascist "economic solution"? Or might it be to go in the opposite direction? To go still further, that is, in the movement of the market, of decoding and deterritorialization? For perhaps the flows are not yet deterritorialized enough, not decoded enough, from the viewpoint of a theory and a practice of a highly schizophrenic character. Not to withdraw from the process, but to go further, to "accelerate the process," as Nietzsche put it: in this matter, the truth is that we haven't seen anything yet (1987, 239–40).

Although there is some ambiguity in this passage (their call to acceleration is couched in a hedging "might it be..."), Deleuze and Guattari clearly signal their sympathy for a revolutionary politics *of the market.* To deal with the oppressions of capitalism by accelerating markets is an admittedly schizophrenic process, hence the title of their two-volume project. Yet as we have also seen, this does not mean a valorization of schizophrenia or some naïve idea about acting schizophrenic. Understanding the schizophrenic nature of modernity is, on the contrary, the key to remaining based — non-reactive, calm, joyous, creative, liberated and liberating. It is only by embracing

97

certain seemingly reactionary affirmations that one enters into connections capable of fomenting collective and aggregate liberations. Based revolutionary politics.

Autocracy and Capital Over Bureaucracy

Power and impotence are not opposites, but correlates. Career bureaucrats gain "power" as they climb the ranks, but this power decreases their freedom of thought and movement. This superficial type of "power" is granted to *compensate* for increasing degrees of impotence. Truly great statesmen, rather, ride historical waves. Nothing is forced. Historical flows, including economic flows, are never themselves a source of domination. Domination or oppression is always traceable to some artifice of institutional capture, installed to channel, divide, tame, or divert the flows.

For anarcho-communist revolutionaries, Deleuze and Guattari have a strange list of favorite statesmen: "Moses the Hebrew, Genseric the Vandal, Genghis the Mongol, Mao the Chinese…" (1987, 296). First of all, Guattari's main political enemies at the time were Maoists, so the mention of Mao does not reflect sympathy for Maoism. Genghis Khan and the Mongols are particularly frequent role models in *Capitalism and Schizophrenia,* although Khan was a genocidal, conquering autocrat. The common virtue of these statesmen is that they rode on historical waves, rather than projecting and enforcing a representation of themselves. They were moved by new ideas, they made new connections, and leveraged new technologies, and thus became expressions of much deeper forces. Their names are only labels for historical dynamics, whereas modern statesmen attempt, feebly, to be their own source of power, to shape historical dynamics. One voter today supports Hillary Clinton because of what Hillary Clinton will do for America, another voter wants Donald Trump because of what he will do for America. But neither of them will do anything for America, because statesmen do not have power over the flows.

For the same reason that a brutal autocrat such as Genghis Khan is preferable to George W. Bush, so too is capital preferable to state-managed

99

bureaucracies. Any institution that pretends to have power *over* the flows is illusory and harmful:

> *...there is no Power regulating the flows themselves. No one dominates the growth of the "monetary mass," or money supply. If an image of the master or an idea of the State is projected outward to the limits of the universe, as if something had domination over flows as well as segments, and in the same manner, the result is a fictitious and ridiculous representation. The stock exchange gives a better image of flows and their quanta than does the State. Capitalists may be the masters of surplus value and its distribution, but they do not dominate the flows from which surplus value derives. Rather, power centers function at the points where flows are converted into segments: they are exchangers, converters, oscillators (1987, 226).*

In short, all the injustices we observe in society — problems of power and domination — are never due to the flows but to the institutions installed onto the flows, the "power centers... where flows are converted into segments." Thus, a certain kind of autocracy may be preferable to liberal democracy, if the autocratic ruler is attuned to the objective flows characterizing world history at the moment. In such cases, the autocrat cannot be said to dominate the people. Similarly, capital may very well be a better ruler than the State, because capitalists never dominate the flows in which they temporarily intervene (as naïve Marxists believe), whereas State bureaucracies are indeed engaged in mad, hopeless attempts to control and even produce the flows.

Following these hints in *Capitalism and Schizophrenia,* we might wonder if their ideal political situation might be an absolute, autocratic sovereign who simply gives free rein to the flows (markets against capitalism). The molecular energies of the people are sufficiently distributed and unleashed, that the autocrat would never bother trying to control them. If such a model were to spread to other polities, the resulting international system would look a lot like Mencius Moldbug's proposal for a patchwork of sovereign corporations (2008).

Chapter Thirteen

The Real, The Evolved, and the Traditional

There is perhaps no better concept to illustrate the chasm between popular Deleuze and Based Deleuze than the infamous "body without organs." This concept sounds like a typical piece of postmodern garbage. But what does it mean? People tend to assume that it involves a creative liberalization. Change your Twitter profile pic to something more mysterious? That's your body without organs. Scribble a strange diagram in your notebook? It depicts your body without organs. Chop off your penis? Body without an organ. In the absence of a strong positive understanding, this is the default meaning imputed to nearly all of Deleuze's most strange and exciting concepts: "Just cut loose, man…"

In fact, the *body without organs*, on the contrary, is a conceptual device for recentering us onto *tradition*.

To understand the body without organs, we must go deeper into the distinction between *actual* and *virtual,* which we first encountered in the chapter *Bearing One's Cross*. Drawing on Spinoza and Henri Bergson, Deleuze makes much of this distinction. Recall that the actual is what most people think of as reality; you're feeling of your body at this moment, the objects in the room around you, etc. The actual is what naïve materialists and Marxists take to be "material reality," or the hard facts. But Bergson showed that, in fact, the actual is not the real. The actual is only a set of arbitrary, contingent, and fleeting circumstances and sensations. The present is always slipping into the past, so whatever is merely actual is no true ground. Rather, what is real is the entire flow of time that leads up to and produces the present. This long continuous flow does not actually exist anywhere, it is virtual, and yet it is the realest of the real.

103

Our sense of the actual is itself biased and misleading due to arbitrary factors of our organisms (Hallward 2006, 61). There are good reasons for us to feel as if the actual present moment is reality — our survival requires it. It is evolutionarily adaptive. But what is useful for one particular organism to think or feel is not the whole picture. As thinking creatures, we are able to reflect on, and discount for, our evolved biases. When we discount for our evolved biases, we intuit that objective reality is intrinsically a virtual reality.

In other words, we falsely perceive the actual, present moment to be true and real, but only because of our particular *organs*. We are nonetheless capable of pursuing, in thought, the counterfactual of what our perceptions would be if we subtracted the bias of our organs. In thought, we can perceive and create *as if* we did not have the organs we have. Notice that this is essentially the scientific method — controlling for biases — but conducted via intuition rather than formalized symbols and measures. These intuitive counterfactuals require some effort and attention, for it is cognitively costly to exit our habit of

104

trusting our organs. Nonetheless, this mental labor is the task *par excellence* of philosophy and science, and any other discipline that seeks to reckon with the real.

To the degree we are able to make ourselves bodies without organs, where exactly will we go, or what exactly will we tend to see? Not some chaotic realm of infinitely unconstrained variety, as the naïve postmodern reading of Deleuze would expect. Rather, the body without organs brings us into consistency with deep time, what Bergson called *pure memory* (Bergson 1988), or what I would call *tradition* — the eternal, uninterrupted line of divine creation, the infinite self-creation of Being.

Reconnecting with deep time is — it turns out — a profound source of creativity. So the postmodern reading of Deleuze is forgivable. But to think that the body without organs is merely a creative violence tearing down the fixed obstacles of the body, would be to miss the point entirely: that it first passes through a highly demanding accountability to the virtual and eternal reality of all that has come before us, and all that will survive us.

Chapter Fourteen

Becoming Minority

The conventional understanding of "minority politics" today is that minorities are marginalized, but they can and should organize to gain power for themselves. Deleuze and Guattari develop a devilish framework that allows them to champion minorities without qualification — in all of his interviews, Deleuze is nothing but sympathetic to the political struggles of minorities — while consistently avoiding the victim-worship that's a common failure mode of bourgeois progressivism. Deleuze and Guattari do not champion minorities per se, they champion "becoming minority," which subtly reverses the conventional narrative connecting marginalization and power. For Deleuze and Guattari, revolution or liberation is not achieved by minorities creating their own power, but by creative people *becoming marginal.*

Deleuze and Guattari distinguish between two types of unconscious social investment. These are two different poles, which is to say that individual cases can be arrayed on a continuum between them. The first pole is paranoiac and fascist, whereas the second pole is schizo and revolutionary. The first pole wants to solidify power, the second pole wants to escape power. I can do no better than Deleuze and Guattari in their crucial and atypically straightforward passage on this matter in *Anti-Oedipus* (Deleuze and Guattari 1983, 277). I quote this passage at length because it also brings together a few other themes of *Based Deleuze*:

> *...first, a paranoiac fascisizing type or pole that invests the formation of central sovereignty; overinvests it by making it the final eternal cause for all the other social forms of history; counterinvests the enclaves or the periphery; and disinvests every free "figure" of desire—yes, I am your kind, and I belong to the superior race and class. And second, a schizorevolutionary type or pole that follows the lines of escape of desire; breaches the wall and causes flows to move;*

assembles its machines and its groups-in-fusion in the enclaves or at the periphery—proceeding in an inverse fashion from that of the other pole: I am not your kind, I belong eternally to the inferior race, I am a beast, a black. Good people say that we must not flee, that to escape is not good, that it isn't effective, and that one must work for reforms. But the revolutionary knows that escape is revolutionary—withdrawal, freaks—provided one sweeps away the social cover on leaving, or causes a piece of the system to get lost in the shuffle. What matters is to break through the wall, even if one has to become black like John Brown. George Jackson. 'I may take flight, but all the while I am fleeing, I will be looking for a weapon!'

Revolutionary politics is an abstract, intensive process but one that produces real effects: a pursuit of one's true calling (a based translation of "desire") away from centralized symbolic focal points, i.e. all mainstream public spectacles, followed by a creative re-attunement of one's cognition on others in the process of escape (the creation of "machines" on the "periphery"). Because the consistency of molar institutions is derived from the statistical regularity of distributed emotions, attitudes, and behaviors, localized instances of "breaking through

108

the wall" *must* produce reverberations on the aggregate social structure. Specifically, these reverberations increase the degrees of freedom within the system, that is, the probability and durability of additional escapes. Revolution is simply the name for the long-run equilibrium of generalized escape dynamics: absolute Freedom if you prefer a left-wing register, or free Absolutism if you prefer a right-wing register. The revolutionary does not negotiate.

Placing all of their bets on "exit" rather than social-democratic "voice," Deleuze and Guattari show their proto-neoreactionary hand in this brilliant passage. You would be hard-pressed to disagree with the political implications of this passage if you were a Peter Thiel, a Nick Land, or a random libertarian seasteader. And yet, they elevate the marginalized while marginalizing the powerful, furnishing us a vitalist, non-resentful, empirically operable radical egalitarianism.

Our currently fashionable anti-racist politics — redistributing power to marginalized groups, through such means as "standing together in solidarity" and so on — is located on the paranoiac-fascist pole. As for the schizo, revolutionary pole, Deleuze and Guattari could not be more provocative. They emphatically affirm that anyone can become minority, become Black, become an Arab, become Woman, become whatever. As they explain in *A Thousand Plateaus*, there can never even be a dominant race: (1987, 379):

> *The race-tribe exists only at the level of an oppressed race, and in the name of the oppression it suffers: there is no race but inferior, minoritarian; there is no dominant race; a race is defined not by its purity but rather by the impurity conferred upon it by a system of domination. Bastard and mixed-blood are the true names of race. Rimbaud said it all on this point: only he or she can invoke race who says, "I have always been of an inferior race... I am of an inferior race for all eternity... There I am on the Breton shore... I am a beast, a nigger... I am of a distant race: my ancestors were Norsemen.*

The subtle genius of this move is that Deleuze and Guattari can be brutally honest and empirically realistic about objective inequalities in traits and abilities — without falling into the trap of racism or fascism. The revolutionary vector is (implicitly) traversed only by those who are *capable* of pursuing their own lines of flight. There is nothing whatsoever in any of their books about teaching escape to those who are unable, waiting for the retarded, etc. No morbid solidarities allowed. But neither are they cruel, or proud, or chauvinist. They know that capabilities are unequally distributed, and uncomfortably correlated with class, gender, race, etc. But by insisting on a tribal-minority aspect within revolutionary liberation, they block any possibility of the disproportionately capable individuals and groups achieving liberation through force. Smart or rich people cannot win by celebrating and affirming their superiority. Deleuze and Guattari are not *objecting,* normatively; they are trying to show that such a pathway can only result in paranoiac alienation and suffering, even and especially for the most capable.

As an aside, the least appreciated achievement of Nick Land's intellectual project to date follows directly from Deleuze and Guattari's paradoxically anti-racist racism. Although it is sadly under-reported, Land's neoreactionary trajectory includes a devastatingly forceful deflation of White

Nationalist fantasies. A whole section of *The Dark Enlightenment* (Land 2012, Part 4) is dedicated to showing that white nationalism is hopeless because today all lines of flight run through exogamy and ethnic diversity in favor of brute intelligence maximization. In true Deleuzian spirit, Land rejects white ethno-nationalist tendencies precisely because "bastard" is the true name of "race:" he mocks white nationalism insofar as it really refers to incest and in-breeding among low-intelligence, uneducated, poor whites. Perhaps his single most infamous and misunderstood piece of writing, a short blog post called *Hyperracism* (Land 2014) expands on this paradoxically anti-racist line of thought. Contemporary racism, he suggests, relies on idiotic and outdated notions that are utterly meaningless compared to the rise of technologically supercharged and planetary-scale assortative mating among the high-IQ and high-income. Disliking black people is retarded at a time when inter-racial marriages of the super intelligent are going to make most normal people obsolete. If Deleuze was able to express an effective "race realism" by running it through the cypher of left-wing rhetoric, Land is expressing an effective anti-racism through the cypher of superficially racist, reactionary rhetoric.

Although it is only implicit, Deleuze and Guattari would affirm that extremely dumb, sad, and/or poor people are generally incapable of escaping or creating anything — if only by ignoring the whole problem so cleverly. But there are perhaps two exceptions to this general rule. One exception is if a person happens to be blessed with exceptional creative stirrings, that compensate for their objective disadvantages. This will be the good fortune of only a very small number of individuals.

A second exception is if the person is adopted or sponsored by someone much smarter, more joyous, wealthier, more based, etc. In some sense, this is the politics Deleuze appears to have practiced toward Guattari. Deleuze's biography is a tranquil desert: though he was inflicted with painful respiratory problems throughout his life, and would ultimately kill himself by the somewhat dramatic method of jumping from a window, there is not much else to observe, other than his thinking, writing, and teaching. He spent his life married to one woman, they had kids, he avoided travel, and avoided

Guattari's constant social, political, and psychiatric happenings. Guattari, in contrast, was a deeply troubled man.[8] He was certainly intelligent, creative, and capable of executing significant work, as he did with his sole-authored books and his activist and psychiatric work. But the man's life was an utter mess, to a degree that has scarcely been confronted by any of the secondary literature. The tragic life of Guattari will provide a sad but fascinating foil for appreciating Deleuze's imperceptibly based vitality.

By his own admission, Guattari "never dared to love his mother... When you lack the courage to love your mother you're condemned to wait endlessly at life's threshold. I'm constantly fleeing the world." When he was nine years old, he had the bad fortune of watching his step-grandfather die of a stroke, which he says triggered a history of severe panic attacks. He initiated many worthy projects, but often in a manic, anxious way, as if to cope with unresolved existential conflicts. He took on too many projects, in a frantic, unrealistic, and self-

---

[8] This section draws liberally from Dosse (2011).

punishing fashion. He was bulimic, a little known fact. He hated the sun and never did anything physical, never played any sports. His second wife reports that he never once swam in the ocean. He was profoundly anxious about death. He once visited a friend with late-stage cancer on his deathbed, and Guattari left the meeting insisting that his friend was "just fine." He was reportedly incapable of completing a stroll through the beautiful, celebrated Père-Lachaise cemetery in Paris.

After first marrying and having three children, he promptly became an absent father, losing himself in huge social groups and always working manically on his various projects. He cheated on his first wife with an intern at his clinic, before finally leaving his wife for the young nurse who possessed a superior, "rich personality." Securing his second wife, he then became a serial womanizer. With the political cover provided by the spirit of the 1960s, he was even a purposeful homewrecker, which he saw as not only defensible but righteous. His second wife eventually left him, which threw him into despair. Unsurprisingly, despair was a recurring feature of his life. His depression was "as spectacular for its profundity as for its length." While we should not blame him for his anxiety and depressiveness, both of which seem largely constitutional, we also should not ignore his repeated and willfully self-destructive patterns of thought and behavior.

In short, I suspect that Deleuze chose to work with Guattari because Guattari was slightly retarded. Guattari was smart, but always falling deep into activist delusions & depressively disordered thinking. Deleuze was leading by example: support and create with the downtrodden, the sad, the failed, and the mentally ill, etc. — just never join their groups. Don't flatter their sins, and do not under any conditions allow yourself to be roped into their clutches.

The very notion of a "Deleuze-Guattari collaboration" must therefore be revised. It was not so much a collaboration as a pedagogical sponsorship by Deleuze, an experiment in tutelage based on a political ethic of Christian charity. Stable genius Deleuze knows privately that this gifted but depressive, womanizing, socially liberal activist is doomed to personal and philosophical dissoluteness, but he — a based husband & father — would turn the boy's ideas into something special.

We find additional corroboration for this view of their relationship insofar as it also explains the exceptionally difficult nature of *Capitalism and Schizophrenia*. They never sought to write impenetrable books, as if they were developing a secret code. Rather, they sought to write a perfectly accessible masterpiece, by radically purifying concepts of their own creation, until those concepts bore no resemblance to anything already existing. Such a venture is never accomplished by proudly mealy-mouthed self-loathing, in the fashion of contemporary white "anti-racist" intellectuals who seem to believe self-flagellation is somehow revolutionary. Consider the first half of a passage we encountered earlier. Imperceptible stammering, through a purification of race (1987, 98), beats perceptible "anti-racism" every time:

> *It was Proust who said that "masterpieces are written in a kind of foreign language." That is the same as stammering, making*

117

language stammer rather than stammering in
speech. To be a foreigner, but in one's own
tongue, not only when speaking a language
other than one's own. To be bilingual,
multilingual, but in one and the same
language, without even a dialect or patois. To
be a bastard, a half-breed, but through a
purification of race.

By refusing to play the pathetic role of worshipping minorities, they realized that if they drilled more radically *into* their particular, idiosyncratic natures (as men, as white men, etc.), the result would be a bizarre admixture that ironically leaves these identity categories behind. White people interested in abolishing white supremacy should *accelerate* their whiteness, rather than maintain it by resentfully suppressing it. White "anti-racists" protect and maintain racial domination because they refuse to own and practice their whiteness to its ultimate, incoherent conclusions. Purifying or accelerating one's race is the only honest and effective way for a member of a dominant race to subvert racial domination and contribute to the empowerment of racial minorities. The result is never "white nationalist" propaganda, but a strange and seemingly impenetrable, bastard language that *confuses* racists and resentful leftists alike (not to mention bourgeois commentators). This bastard language is only ever interesting or useful to others who are also converging on the smooth open spaces of liberated creativity. Again, the case of Nick Land is instructive: the most original and effective anti-White-Nationalist philosophy as of 2019 was created through a philosophy blog that no journalist or academic can understand, by a white British man who journalists and academics consider racist. His bastard philosophy makes the language of white racism stammer, from Shanghai no less…

Capitalism and Schizophrenia has nothing to hide, but if you are so mentally pacified that your only method of reading new books is to relate them to previous books, then you'll find *Capitalism and Schizophrenia* impenetrable. That is the type of person they are hiding from. If you allow the work to generate its own immanent coherence, without requiring or expecting it to slot sensibly into your pre-existing schemas, then you will find its system surprisingly logical and transparent. In this work,

Deleuze was learning how to free himself from his own success and social status, learning how to become marginal, learning how to become a bastard, by becoming a foreigner in his own tongue. They were trying to demonstrate the "straight and narrow path," not *between* the Right and Left (as if they were centrists) but *out of* both paranoiac right-wing Fascism and resentful, left-wing Socialism.

Acknowledgments

I would like to thank my based parents, Caroline and Kevin Murphy, for not having an abortion and never getting divorced. I would also like to thank Jeff Bergen, Johnny Blaze, Jacob Lyles, and Brenton Milne for their generous support.

References

There are many good resources on Gilles Deleuze, most of which did not need to be cited for this book. To find more books, podcasts, and videos on Deleuze, see my curated list of resources at: theotherlifenow.com/deleuze-resources.

Althusser, Louis. 1990. *For Marx*. London New York: Verso.

Althusser, Louis, and Étienne Balibar. 2009. *Reading Capital: The Complete Edition*. London: Verso.

Berger, Edmund. 2017. "Deleuze, Guattari and Market Anarchism." *Center for a Stateless Society*. https://c4ss.org/content/47692.

Bergson, Henri. 1988. *Matter and Memory*. New York: Zone Books.

Braudel, Fernand. 1982. *The Wheels of Commerce: Civilization & Capitalism*

15th-18th Century, Volume 2. New York: Harper & Row, Publishers.

Brickman, Philip, Dan Coates, and Ronnie Janoff-Bulman. 1978. "Lottery Winners and Accident Victims: Is Happiness Relative?" *Journal of Personality and Social Psychology* 36 (8): 917.

Carl, Noah. 2019. "Noah Carl Controversy: FAQ." *Medium*. https://blog.usejournal.com/noah-carl-controversy-faq-ad967834b12d.

Crawford, Lucas Cassidy. 2008. "Transgender Without Organs? Mobilizing a Geo-Affective Theory of Gender Modification." *Women's Studies Quarterly* 36 (3/4): 127–43. https://www.jstor.org/stable/27649790.

Deleuze, Gilles. 1968. *Difference and Repetition*. New York: Columbia University Press.

———. 1986. *Cinema 1: The Movement-Image*. Minneapolis: University of Minnesota.

———. 1995. *Negotiations, 1972-1990*. New York: Columbia University Press.

———. 2006. *Nietzsche and Philosophy*. London: Continuum.

———. 1946. "From Christ to the Bourgeoisie." Translated by Raymond van de Wiel, December, 1–7. http://documents.raymondvandewiel.org/from_christ_to_the_bourgeoisie_translation.pdf.

Deleuze, Gilles, and Félix Guattari. 1986. *Kafka: Toward a Minor Literature*. Minneapolis: University of Minnesota Press.

———. 1987. *A Thousand Plateaus*. Translated by Brian Massumi. Minneapolis: University of Minnesota Press.

———. 1994. *What Is Philosophy*. Translated by Hugh Tomlinson and Graham Burchell. New York: Columbia University Press.

———. 1983. *Anti-Oedipus*. Translated by Robert Hurley, Mark Seem, and Helen R. Lane. Minneapolis: University of Minnesota Press.

Deleuze, Gilles, and Claire Parnet. 2002. *Dialogues II*. Translated by Hugh Tomlinson and Barbara Habberjam. New York: Columbia University Press.

Deleuze, Gilles, and Leopold von Sacher-Masoch. 1989. *Masochism: Coldness and Cruelty & Venus in Furs*. New York: Zone Books.

Doel, Marcus A. 2002. "Un-Glunking Geography: Spatial Science After Dr. Seuss and Gilles Deleuze." In *Thinking Space*, edited by M. Crang and N. Thrift. Critical Geographies. London: Taylor & Francis. https://books.google.com/books?id=oNGEAgAAQBAJ.

Dosse, François. 2011. *Gilles Deleuze & Félix Guattari: Intersecting Lives*. Translated by Deborah Glassman. New York: Columbia University Press.

Emma, Renold, and David Mellor. 2013. "Deleuze and Guattari in the Nursery: Towards an Ethnographic, Multi-Sensory Mapping of Gendered Bodies and Becomings." In *Deleuze and Research Methodologies*, edited by

Rebecca Coleman. Deleuze Connections EUP.
Edinburgh: Edinburgh University Press.

Goodley, Dan. 2007. "Becoming Rhizomatic
Parents: Deleuze, Guattari and Disabled
Babies." *Disability & Society* 22 (2): 145–60.
https://doi.org/10.1080/09687590601141576.

Hallward, Peter. 2006. *Out of This World:
Deleuze and the Philosophy of Creation.*
London: Verso.

Hatemi, Peter K., Sarah E. Medland, Robert
Klemmensen, Sven Oskarrson, Levente Littvay,
Chris Dawes, Brad Verhulst, et al. 2014.
"Genetic Influences on Political Ideologies:
Twin Analyses of 19 Measures of Political
Ideologies from Five Democracies and
Genome-Wide Findings from Three
Populations." *Behavior Genetics* 44 (3): 282–
94. https://doi.org/10.1007/s10519-014-9648-8.

Herrnstein, Richard, and Murray, Charles.
1996. *The Bell Curve: Intelligence and Class
Structure in American Life.* New York: Simon
& Schuster.

Hickey-Moody, Anna, and Denise Wood. 2008. "Virtually Sustainable: Deleuze and Desiring Differenciation in Second Life." *Continuum* 22 (6): 805–16. https://doi.org/ 10.1080/10304310802452479.

Holland, Eugene. 2011. *Nomad Citizenship: Free-Market Communism and the Slow-Motion General Strike*. Minneapolis: University of Minnesota Press.

Inbar, Yoel, David A. Pizarro, and Paul Bloom. 2009. "Conservatives Are More Easily Disgusted Than Liberals." *Cognition and Emotion* 23 (4): 714–25. https://doi.org/ 10.1080/02699930802110007.

Jean-François Lyotard. 1990. *Pérégrinations: Loi, Forme, événement*. Paris: Galilée.

LaFinta, Sim. 2004. "Metaprogramming as Anacalypsis in an Age of Auto-Generated Trolls and Daemons." *Aerospace Medicine and Human Performance* 33 (2). https:// www.nasa.gov/centers/hq/library.

Land, Nick. 1993. "Machinic Desire." *Textual Practice* 7 (3): 471–82. https://doi.org/10.1080/09502369308582177.

———. 2012. "The Dark Enlightenment." http://www.thedarkenlightenment.com/the-dark-enlightenment-by-nick-land/.

———. 2013. "Re-Accelerationism." *Outside In*. http://www.xenosystems.net/re-accelerationism/.

———. 2014. "Hyper-Racism." *Outside In*. http://www.xenosystems.net/hyper-racism/.

May, Todd. 2005. *Gilles Deleuze: An Introduction*. Cambridge, UK: Cambridge University Press.

Miller, DC, and Justin Murphy. 2019. "The Rectification of Names with DC Miller: On Conservatives, Fascists, NRx and Free-Speech Leftism." *Other Life*. https://theotherlifenow.com/the-rectification-of-names-with-dc-miller/.

Moldbug, Mencius. 2007. "How Dawkins Got Pwned." *Unqualified Reservations*. https://

www.unqualified-reservations.org/2007/09/
how-dawkins-got-pwned-part-1/.

———. 2008. "Patchwork: A Political System
for the 21st Century." *Unqualified
Reservations*. https://www.unqualified-
reservations.org/2008/11/patchwork-positive-
vision-part-1/.

Murphy, Justin. 2017a. "Capitalism Is an
Instance, Not an Essence." *Jmrphy.net*. https://
jmrphy.net/blog/2017/04/28/capitalism-is-an-
instance/.

———. 2017b. "On Turning Left into
Darkness." *Jmrphy.net*. https://jmrphy.net/blog/
2017/04/11/on-turning-left-into-darkness/.

———. 2018a. "Atomization and Liberation."
Vast Abrupt. https://vastabrupt.com/
2018/01/07/atomization-and-liberation/.

———. 2018b. "Fascism over Yourself Is
Called Autonomy." *Other Life*. https://
theotherlifenow.com/fascism-over-yourself-is-
called-autonomy/.

———. 2018c. "Reality Patchwork and Neo-Feudal Techno-Communism." *Other Life*. https://theotherlifenow.com/on-reality-patchwork-and-neo-feudal-techno-communism/.

Murphy, Justin, and Johannes Niederhauser. 2019. "Heidegger, Ecstatic Time, & the Community of Mortals." https://www.youtube.com/watch?v=ooN1IL06jxc.

Negri, Antonio, and Gilles Deleuze. 1990. "Gilles Deleuze in Conversation with Antonio Negri." *Futur Anterieur* 1. http://www.generation-online.org/p/fpdeleuze3.htm.

Peterson, Jordan B, and Shelley Carson. 2000. "Latent Inhibition and Openness to Experience in a High- Achieving Student Population." *Personality and Individual Differences* 28 (2). https://doi.org/10.1016/S0191-8869(99)00101-4.

Peterson, Jordan B, Kathleen W Smith, and Shelley Carson. 2002. "Openness and Extraversion Are Associated with Reduced Latent Inhibition: Replication and

Commentary." *Personality and Individual Differences* 33 (7): 1137–47.

Potts, Annie. 2004. "Deleuze on Viagra (or, What Can a 'Viagra-Body' Do?)." *Body & Society* 10 (1): 17–36. https://doi.org/10.1177/1357034X04041759.

Poulous, James. 2005. "Hunter Thompson's Reactionary Heart." *The American Spectator*. https://spectator.org/48677_hunter-thompsons-reactionary-heart/.

Reynolds, Jack. 2006. "Sadism and Masochism — A Symptomatology of Analytic and Continental Philosophy?" *Parrhesia* 1. https://www.parrhesiajournal.org/parrhesia01/parrhesia01_reynolds.pdf.

Schnall, Simone, Jonathan Haidt, Gerald L. Clore, and Alexander H. Jordan. 2008. "Disgust as Embodied Moral Judgment." *Personality and Social Psychology Bulletin* 34 (8): 1096–1109. https://doi.org/10.1177/0146167208317771.

Smith, Daniel, and John Protevi. 2018. "Gilles Deleuze." In *The Stanford Encyclopedia of*

Philosophy, edited by Edward N. Zalta, Spring 2018. Metaphysics Research Lab, Stanford University. https://plato.stanford.edu/archives/spr2018/entries/deleuze/.

Sullivan, Sian. 2010. "'Ecosystem Service Commodities' - A New Imperial Ecology? Implications for Animist Immanent Ecologies, with Deleuze and Guattari." *New Formations*, no. 69: 111–28. https://doi.org/10.3898/NEWF.69.06.2010.

Sørensen, Bent Meier. 2005. "Immaculate Defecation: Gilles Deleuze and Félix Guattari in Organization Theory." *The Sociological Review* 53 (1): 120–33. https://doi.org/10.1111/j.1467-954X.2005.00545.x.

Wiel, Raymond van de. 2010. "From Christ to the Bourgeoisie: Deleuze, Spiritualism, Sartre and the World." *Raymondvandewiel.org*. https://raymondvandewiel.org/post/127463632357/from-christ-to-the-bourgeoisie-deleuze.

Wilson, Edward O. 1975. *Sociobiology: The New Synthesis*. Cambridge, Mass: Belknap Press of Harvard University Press.

Wolters, Eugene. 2013. "13 Things You Didn't Know About Deleuze and Guattari." *Critical-Theory.com*. http://www.critical-theory.com/deleuze-guattari-biography/.